W9-CNA-161

Preparing Students for

Grade

Standardized Testing 5

By
JANET P. SITTER, Ph.D.

COPYRIGHT © 2004 Mark Twain Media, Inc.

ISBN 1-58037-267-8

Printing No. CD-1627

Mark Twain Media, Inc., Publishers
Distributed by Carson-Dellosa Publishing Company, Inc.

Table of Contents

Test Lessons:

Table of Contents (cont.)

Introduction

Standardized tests are designed to measure how well a student has learned the basic knowledge and skills that are taught in elementary and middle schools. They generally cover the content areas of reading, vocabulary, language, spelling, math, science, and social studies. The most recent standardized tests also focus on the student's ability to think critically. It would be unrealistic, however, to expect that students will know (or have been taught) all of the material on the tests. Some of this material will be new to students, and this may cause anxiety in both students and teachers.

The purpose of this book is to help you familiarize your students with the format and language of tests, with important test-taking strategies, and with practice in the content areas of the major standardized tests used nationally. These include:

- ✏ **The California Achievement Tests (CAT/5)**

- ✏ **The Iowa Tests of Basic Skills (ITBS)**

- ✏ **The Comprehensive Tests of Basic Skills (CTBS)**

- ✏ **The Stanford Achievement Tests (SAT)**

- ✏ **The Metropolitan Achievement Tests (MAT)**

- ✏ **The Texas Assessment of Academic Skills (TAAS)**

By spending 20 minutes a day for three weeks prior to the administration of the standardized test for your school district and grade level and using the material in this book, you will not only increase your students' confidence in their test-taking skills but also help them to successfully demonstrate their knowledge and skills. *Preparing Students for Standardized Testing* will provide your students with opportunities to take practice tests under similar conditions to those that exist on standardized tests. Teachers should photocopy the practice tests in the book and the practice answer sheets for students to use. This will familiarize students with the process of filling in computer-scored answer sheets. In order to better prepare your students for standardized testing, it may be beneficial to set a time limit you think is appropriate for the average student in your class.

Content Area Skills

READING

Word Analysis:
- ✔ Identify prefixes, suffixes, root words
- ✔ Recognize figurative language
- ✔ Demonstrate knowledge of structural relationships in letters, words, signs

Vocabulary:
- ✔ Identify synonyms, antonyms, homophones, palindromes
- ✔ Recognize word origins and words in context
- ✔ Demonstrate knowledge of multiple meanings of words

Comprehension:
- ✔ Identify main idea and supporting details
- ✔ Recognize theme, story elements, and author's purpose
- ✔ Demonstrate literal/interpretive understanding
- ✔ Distinguish cause/effect, reality/fantasy
- ✔ Demonstrate critical understanding by drawing conclusions, making predictions, and extending meaning to other contexts

LANGUAGE

Mechanics:
- ✔ Identify the appropriate use of capitalization, punctuation, and parts of speech in text
- ✔ Recognize correct spelling in text
- ✔ Identify misspelled words in text

Expression:
- ✔ Identify topic, concluding, and supporting sentences in text
- ✔ Determine correct usage, sequence of ideas, and relevance of information
- ✔ Recognize connective/transitional words, phrases, and sentences
- ✔ Identify and correct errors in existing text and in text written by student

Information Skills:
- ✔ Identify parts of a book
- ✔ Recognize and use dictionary and other reference materials
- ✔ Demonstrate ability to understand and interpret maps, charts, and diagrams

Content Area Skills (cont.)

<u>MATHEMATICS</u>

Concepts:
- ✔ Identify, compare, and order numbers and number operations
- ✔ Recognize and compare equivalent numbers
- ✔ Interpret and apply numbers in real-world situations
- ✔ Demonstrate knowledge of estimation, place value, expanded notation, rounding, Roman numerals, time, geometric shapes and planes, rays, angles, parallel, and perpendicular

Computation:
- ✔ Identify the properties and relationships of numbers and operations
- ✔ Recognize and extend patterns, transformations, symmetry, and geometric figures
- ✔ Recognize and solve real-world computation problems
- ✔ Demonstrate proficiency in computation procedures in addition, subtraction, multiplication, division, decimals, and fractions

Problem Solving and Reasoning:
- ✔ Identify and apply problem-solving strategies to real-world problems
- ✔ Recognize and interpret data in models, diagrams, pictures, graphs
- ✔ Use a variety of estimation strategies; determine reasonableness of results
- ✔ Demonstrate inductive/deductive reasoning and spatial and proportional reasoning to solve real-world problems

<u>SCIENCE</u>

Process and Inquiry:
- ✔ Identify scientific principles, processes, and inquiry
- ✔ Interpret and make reasonable interpretations from scientific data
- ✔ Recognize use of inferences to draw conclusions
- ✔ Demonstrate an understanding of fundamental concepts of scientific inquiry

Concepts:
- ✔ Identify life cycles of plants and animals; understand the term *habitat*
- ✔ Understand water cycle, terms *decomposers, fossil fuel, eclipse, buoyancy*
- ✔ Understand societal issues such as recycling and pollution
- ✔ Recognize basic principles of earth (e.g. rocks, minerals, earthquakes, volcanoes) and space (e.g. air, planets, solar systems)
- ✔ Demonstrate knowledge of basic health and nutrition for the human body

Content Area Skills (cont.)

<u>SOCIAL STUDIES</u>

History and Cultures:

✔ Identify famous people, holidays, symbols, customs, norms, and social institutions in the United States and connect historical events to them
✔ Recognize the contributions, influences, and interactions of various cultures
✔ Recognize patterns of similarities in different historical times
✔ Use time lines, product and global maps, and cardinal directions
✔ Demonstrate an historical understanding of time, continuity, and societal change in the United States and the world

Civics, Government, and Economics:

✔ Identify government bodies, levels of government, and characteristics of good citizenship
✔ Recognize the roles and responsibilities of government and citizens; recognize important documents
✔ Demonstrate an understanding of the basic principles of government
✔ Understand the democratic process
✔ Identify economic principles of supply/demand, consumer/producer, goods/ services, profit/loss
✔ Recognize three roles individuals play: worker, consumer, citizen
✔ Understand economic concepts related to products, jobs, and the environment

Geography:

✔ Identify and use geographic terms to describe land forms, bodies of water, weather, and climate
✔ Demonstrate geographic methods to interpret maps, graphs, charts, photographs
✔ Understand global and environmental issues
✔ Locate continents, major countries, resources, and regions

The Language of Tests

Here are some of the most frequently used terms in assessment.

Accountability: The practice of evaluating teachers and schools based on measurable goals

Achievement Test: Tests designed to measure knowledge and skills, usually objective, standardized, and norm-referenced

Alternative Assessment: Methods of evaluating student work and progress that are *not* traditional standardized tests (e.g., portfolios, anecdotal records, teacher observation, interviews, performance, demonstration projects, etc.)

Assessment: A systematic method for testing student progress and achievement

Authentic Assessment: The tasks and procedures used for assessment are closely related to tasks found in the real world.

Content Validity: The extent to which the content of a test actually measures the knowledge and skills the test claims to measure

Criterion-referenced Test: A test that measures a student's performance to a predetermined measure of success, rather than to a norm group

Curricular Validity: The extent to which a test measures what has been taught

Diagnostic Test: A test used to assess specific characteristics in order to make instructional decisions

Evaluation: The process of making judgments and instructional decisions obtained from a form of assessment

Grade Equivalent Score: A measure that compares a student's raw score on a standardized test to average scores across grade levels

Group Test: A test that is administered to more than one student at the same time

Individual Test: A test that is administered to only one student at a time

Intelligence Test: A test that measures a student's general mental ability or scholastic aptitude

Mean: The average of a set of test scores

Median: The middle score of a set of test scores

Minimum-competency Test: A test that measures whether a student has attained the minimum level of overall achievement necessary for a particular purpose

The Language of Tests (cont.)

Mode: The most frequent score of a group of scores

National Standards: A set of standards for an entire country, usually including content standards, performance standards, and school standards

Norm Group: The group whose test performance is used to establish levels of performance on a standardized test

Norm-referenced Test: A test that measures the student's score with the average performance of all test takers

Objective Test: A test in which each question is stated in such a way that there is only one correct answer

Percentage Score: The percentage of correct responses on a test

Percentile Score: Proportion of other students' scores that equal or fall below a given student's score

Population: A complete set of students to which a set of test results will be generalized

Portfolio Assessment: Collecting children's work on an ongoing basis and examining it for evidence of growth

Raw Score: The number of correct responses on a test

Reliability: The consistency in test results or the degree to which a test's results actually measure what a student can do

Rubric: A scoring guide based on a scale for rating a group of students

Standardized Test: A test with specific procedures so that comparable measures may be made by testers in different geographic areas

Test Anxiety: Nervous energy felt by test-takers; sharpens the mind

Test Bias: Tendency for a test to be unfair for students in some groups but not in others

Validity: The degree to which a test measures what it is designed to measure

Writing Assessment: A test in which students are asked to demonstrate writing abilities by actually writing in response to given prompts

Writing Prompt: A question or statement to which the test-taker is asked to respond

Overview of Testing Tips

- Read (or listen) to directions carefully.

- Follow all instructions, including icons.

- Read the entire question.

- Read all answer choices before picking one.

- Budget your time wisely.

- Do not spend too much time on any one question.

- Use all of the time provided; testing is not the same as a race.

- Pay close attention to how the question is written.

- Avoid making answer sheet errors.

- Skip hard questions, and answer the easy ones first.

- Use the process of elimination to find answers.

- Use logical reasoning to choose the best answer.

- When all else fails, guess.

- Answer all test questions.

- Think twice before changing an answer.

- Control test anxiety.

- Stay calm and focus on the task at hand.

Important Terms and Concepts

It might be helpful to review the following terms and concepts with the students prior to taking the practice tests.

Reading
comprehension
fantasy
fable
folk tale
poetry
alliteration
personification
oxymoron
figurative language
characters
setting
context clues
proverbs
main idea/supporting details

Language Arts
synonym
antonym
analogy
palindrome
homophone
pronoun
topic sentence
supporting details
syllables
combining sentences
subject
predicate
capitalization
punctuation
web addresses (zones)
encyclopedias
dictionaries
libraries
Standard English
table of contents
glossary
maps, map key
webs

Math
symmetry
congruent
intersect
least common multiple
diameter
radius
volume
place value
Roman numerals
multiples
average
measurement
stopwatch
thermometer
addition
subtraction
multiplication
division
mathematician
less than
greater than
equal to
area
perimeter
fraction
simplest form
line
grid

Science
decomposers
fossil fuel
eclipse
buoyancy
carnivore
chlorophyll
food chain
herbivore
omnivore

photosynthesis
learned behavior
instinct
density
gravity
mass
volume
weight
planet
probe
rocky planet
frozen planet
telescope

Social Studies

History and Culture
multicultural
continent
country
region
famous explorers
famous monuments
time line
Lewis and Clark
Trail of Tears
astronauts
charts, maps, grids, graphs
Pearl Harbor
Twin Towers
United Nations
Wright Brothers
Thurgood Marshall
Neil Armstrong
Sally Ride
John Glenn
Condoleeza Rice
Colin Powell
Martin Luther King, Jr.

Important Terms and Concepts (cont.)

Civics, Government, Economics

goods
services
economy
consumer
producer
supply
demand
democracy
dictatorship
monarchy
Bill of Rights
Declaration of Independence
U.S. Constitution
legislative branch
executive branch
judicial branch
Senate
House of Representatives
governor
mayor
commander-in-chief
Ellis Island
Angel Island
immigrants

Geography

landforms
landmarks
maps, charts, graphs, grids
compass rose
political map
topographical map
population map
climate map
resource map
states
regions
directions
major rivers
Amazon
Rio Grande
Gulf of Mexico
Caribbean Sea

Hi! Whenever you see me, I'll give you some testing tips to help with your test-taking skills.

Filling Out the Answer Sheet

The first thing you will do during standardized testing is to correctly fill out your answer sheet. Below is an example of an answer sheet. The circles must be filled in for every box, so for empty boxes, fill in the empty circles. Use a No. 2 pencil, so the computer can score your answer sheet. Fill in your circles completely, and fill in only one for each question. If you erase an answer, be sure that you erase it completely before filling in your new choice. The computer will mark wrong any question that seems to have more than one choice marked. Erase all stray pencil marks on the page.

Practice filling out this sample form with your name. Print your name in the boxes at the top. Then darken the circle for that letter in the column under each letter. For blank spaces, darken the blank circles.

Filling Out the Answer Sheet (cont.)

Practice filling out this sample form with your birth date, gender, and grade. Print your teacher's name, school name, and district in the boxes at the top. Then darken the circles for your birth date, gender, and grade.

TEACHER
SCHOOL
DISTRICT

BIRTH DATE

Month	Day		Year	
Jan ○	⓪	⓪	⓪	⓪
Feb ○	①	①		①
Mar ○	②	②		②
Apr ○	③	③		③
May ○		④		④
Jun ○		⑤		⑤
Jul ○		⑥		⑥
Aug ○		⑦	⑦	⑦
Sep ○		⑧	⑧	⑧
Oct ○		⑨	⑨	⑨
Nov ○				
Dec ○				

GENDER

○ Female   ○ Male

GRADE

③   ④   ⑤   ⑥   ⑦   ⑧

Helpful Reading Strategies

Test Tips

1. Read <u>all</u> directions carefully.
2. Be sure you understand the directions.
3. Read <u>all</u> answer choices before selecting one.
4. Format changes may <u>not</u> signal a change in directions; don't be tricked.
5. Look for the key words in the directions.
6. Skip difficult items and come back to them.
7. Read back over your test to be sure you answered all questions.
8. If you aren't sure which answer is correct, take your best guess.

Reading Strategies

★ When reading comprehension is tested, the questions are testing your ability to read for details and to find meaning in the text.

★ When you are looking for the main idea of a selection, look at the first sentence, the last sentence, or the title. These usually provide a good clue as to the main idea.

★ When the directions say choose the *"most important idea,"* or *"the main problem,"* remember that there is probably more than one right answer. You need to look for the BEST answer.

★ When you are trying to figure out a vocabulary word from context, replace the word with the answer and see if it fits.

★ Watch out for negatives. Some questions say, *"which of the following **is not** true?".* You are looking for the one that is wrong (false).

★ Use context clues to figure out words or ideas you don't understand.

★ Word-meaning questions test your vocabulary and your ability to figure out unfamiliar words.

Name: _____ Date: _____

UNIT ONE: READING

Lesson One: Vocabulary

> **Directions:** Read the series of compound word beginnings or endings, and then choose a word that completes each word.

1. _____ bird, _____ board, _____ smith
   A. head   B. snow   C. black   D. arrow

2. water _____, rain _____, wind _____
   A. fall   B. mark   C. bow   D. mill

3. gun _____, hot _____, pot _____
   A. boat   B. shot   C. sight   D. hole

4. _____ walk, _____ roads, _____ word
   A. side   B. cross   C. rain   D. hot

> **Directions:** Choose the word in each group of words that does not belong.

5. A. extinct
   B. microscopic
   C. petite
   D. small

6. A. old
   B. ancient
   C. antique
   D. inattentive

7. A. brave
   B. cowardly
   C. courageous
   D. bold

8. A. hate
   B. like
   C. enjoy
   D. fancy

9. A. happy
   B. cheerful
   C. sad
   D. glad

10. A. heap
    B. mound
    C. pile
    D. conceal

Read all directions carefully.

Name: _____ Date: _____

Lesson One: Vocabulary (cont.)

Directions: Choose the antonym for each word.

---

11. **wild**
    - A.   laugh
    - B.   tame
    - C.   poor
    - D.   agony

12. **moan**
    - A.   groan
    - B.   soothe
    - C.   comfort
    - D.   laugh

13. **drag**
    - A.   tow
    - B.   pull
    - C.   push
    - D.   haul

14. **join**
    - A.   separate
    - B.   connect
    - C.   link
    - D.   unite

15. **frigid**
    - A.   frosty
    - B.   hot
    - C.   icy
    - D.   chilly

Directions: Choose the word that best completes the sentence.

---

16. Carol's _____ tops never match her bottoms.
    - A.   cuisine   B.   tattoo   C.   travois   D.   pajama

17. My brother took eighth grade _____ and hated it.
    - A.   travois   B.   assassin   C.   algebra   D.   shampoo

18. The near-sighted _____ missed his target.
    - A.   travois   B.   assassin   C.   algebra   D.   shampoo

19. The men used a(n) _____ to carry their friend out of the woods.
    - A.   travois   B.   assassin   C.   algebra   D.   shampoo

20. My parents went to a fancy restaurant for its fine _____.
    - A.   cuisine   B.   assassin   C.   shampoo   D.   exotic

Name: _____ Date: _____

Lesson One: Vocabulary (cont.)

Directions: Decide which word is most similar in meaning to the word in **bold** type.

21. After my foot surgery, I had to **elevate** my feet each day.
    A. avert   B. bare   C. raise   D. heed

22. Olive was always in trouble for being such a **chatterbox**.
    A. parrot   B. talker   C. clown   D. mystery

23. Sam's parents were again **dissatisfied** with his academic progress.
    A. inconsiderate   B. ferocious   C. critical   D. unhappy

24. Danny was **furious** with Matt for breaking his bicycle.
    A. amazed   B. very angry   C. dazed   D. exhausted

25. The bakery's new neon sign **illuminates** the whole neighborhood.
    A. lights up   B. ignores   C. fouls   D. motivates

Directions: Read each pair of word meanings. Choose the word that fits both meanings.

26. a strip of sticky material
    to record
    A. write
    B. photograph
    C. tape
    D. measure

27. a flying animal
    a club used to hit a ball
    A. squirrel
    B. bat
    C. stick
    D. birdy

28. a steep bank or cliff
    to fool or to mislead
    A. bluff
    B. hill
    C. trick
    D. mountain

29. a business or company
    solid or hard
    A. team
    B. group
    C. tough
    D. firm

30. a direction
    went away
    A. left
    B. right
    C. gone
    D. here

31. building used for worship
    side of the forehead
    A. temple
    B. church
    C. synagogue
    D. chin

Name: _____ Date: _____

Lesson One: Vocabulary (cont.)

Directions: Complete the analogy by choosing the best answer.

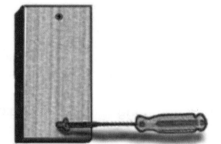

32. *screw* is to *screwdriver* as *nail* is to _____
    A. drive
    B. hammer
    C. pound
    D. tack

33. *freeze* is to *solid* as *melt* is to _____
    A. liquid
    B. ice
    C. heat
    D. evaporate

34. *win* is to *lose* as *victory* is to _____
    A. contest
    B. compete
    C. award
    D. defeat

35. *rain* is to *snow* as *dew* is to _____
    A. frost
    B. cloud
    C. ground
    D. ice

Directions: Read this passage, and then decide which word best fits each blank.

Tiny hummingbirds are among the __36__ birds in the world. They are only found in the Western __37__. Nineteen varieties of the 320 species live in __38__ America. The tiniest hummingbird, less than 2 inches (5 cm) long, is the bee __39__ of Cuba.

Hummingbirds can beat their __40__ up to 70 times per second. This is what causes their distinctive __41__ sound. It also allows hummingbirds to __42__ in midair and to fly backward and sideways like helicopters. In this way, the birds __43__ from flower to flower and feed while flying. They drink the sweet nectar and eat tiny __44__ from deep within the cups of __45__.

Name: _____ Date: _____

Lesson One: Vocabulary (cont.)

36. A.   smallest   B.   ugliest   C.   rarest   D.   best

37. A.   World   B.   America   C.   Hemisphere   D.   Caribbean

38. A.   North   B.   colonial   C.   warm   D.   West

39. A.   stinger   B.   bird   C.   bat   D.   hummingbird

40. A.   arms   B.   legs   C.   wings   D.   beaks

41. A.   humming   B.   singing   C.   whistling   D.   rhyming

42. A.   fly   B.   hover   C.   tread   D.   flow

43. A.   fly   B.   dart   C.   dig   D.   hum

44. A.   worms   B.   slugs   C.   flies   D.   insects

45. A.   weeds   B.   grass   C.   flowers   D.   bushes

Name: _____ Date: _____

UNIT ONE: READING

Lesson Two: Word Analysis

Directions: Read the word with the underlined letter or letters, and then choose the word that has the same sound.

Be sure that you understand the directions.

1. cl<u>ou</u>d
   - A. toupee
   - B. juice
   - C. found
   - D. fruit

2. b<u>oy</u>
   - A. down
   - B. okra
   - C. cry
   - D. loyalty

3. <u>th</u>ree
   - A. bother
   - B. smooth
   - C. toothbrush
   - D. mother

4. law<u>y</u>er
   - A. quickly
   - B. sky
   - C. baby
   - D. yonder

5. d<u>aw</u>n
   - A. gave
   - B. path
   - C. caught
   - D. pray

6. <u>u</u>kulele
   - A. plum
   - B. bump
   - C. puke
   - D. rub

Directions: Read the word, and then choose the word that does <u>not</u> have the same sound as the underlined letter or letters.

7. <u>g</u>ym
   - A. gem
   - B. giraffe
   - C. gang
   - D. giant

8. <u>c</u>ity
   - A. cent
   - B. carpet
   - C. cycle
   - D. scent

9. <u>s</u>un
   - A. sale
   - B. sit
   - C. sure
   - D. send

10. <u>gh</u>ost
   - A. ghetto
   - B. ghastly
   - C. ghoul
   - D. rough

Name: _____ Date: _____

Lesson Two: Word Analysis (cont.)

11. <u>ph</u>one
   A.   phonics   B.   bought   C.   laugh   D.   farmer

12. <u>ch</u>ain
   A.   chorus   B.   cheese   C.   church   D.   chick

13. ro<u>s</u>e
   A.   cookies   B.   boys   C.   soup   D.   please

Directions: Read the word, and then decide which of the choices can be added to form a compound word.

14. grown _____
   A.   up
   B.   down
   C.   old
   D.   tired

> Format changes <u>may</u> <u>not</u> signal changes in directions, so don't be fooled!

15. _____ place
   A.   first   B.   my   C.   fire   D.   John's

16. air _____
   A.   Jordan   B.   plane   C.   cloud   D.   crowd

17. _____ fish
   A.   one   B.   go   C.   ugly   D.   star

18. watch _____
   A.   football   B.   wrist   C.   me   D.   dog

Directions: Choose the root word for each word.

19. perimeter
   A.   peri
   B.   meter
   C.   perim
   D.   rimeter

20. rebellion
   A.   rebel
   B.   lion
   C.   rebe
   D.   bellion

> Look for key words in the directions ... like <u>root</u> <u>word</u>, for example.

Name: _____ Date: _____

Lesson Two: Word Analysis (cont.)

21. courageous
    A. age
    B. cour
    C. courage
    D. ous

22. geography
    A. geog
    B. graph
    C. graphy
    D. geo

23. television
    A. vis
    B. tel
    C. tele
    D. vision

24. microscope
    A. mic
    B. scope
    C. micro
    D. cros

25. bicycle
    A. bi
    B. cycle
    C. bic
    D. icy

Directions: Choose the prefix for each word.

---

26. anteroom
    A. ant
    B. ante
    C. room
    D. om

27. nonfiction
    A. tion
    B. fict
    C. non
    D. fiction

28. Internet
    A. In
    B. Inter
    C. net
    D. ternet

29. megaphone
    A. meg
    B. mega
    D. phone
    D. gaph

30. ambidextrous
    A. am
    B. bidex
    C. ambi
    D. rous

Directions: Choose the suffix for each word.

---

31. friendship
    A. friend
    B. ship
    C. fri
    D. end

32. motherly
    A. moth
    B. other
    C. ther
    D. ly

If you aren't sure which answer is correct, then guess.

Name: _____   Date: _____

Lesson Two: Word Analysis (cont.)

33.   American
A.   can   B.   an   C.   rican   D.   merican

34.   clockwise
A.   clock   B.   kwise   C.   ock   D.   wise

35.   metallic
A.   met   B.   tall   C.   ic   D.   tallic

Directions: Choose the correct way to divide each word into syllables.

---

36.   A.   pict - ure
B.   pic - tu - re
C.   pi - cture
D.   pic - ture

37.   A.   ar - ticle
B.   a - rti - cle
C.   ar - ti - cle
D.   art - i - cle

38.   A.   aud - ie - nce
B.   au - di - ence
C.   aud - i - en - ce
D.   aud - i - ence

39.   A.   po - li - o
B.   pol - i - o
C.   po - lio
D.   pol - io

40.   A.   spec - tac - u - lar
B.   spectac - ular
C.   spectac - u - lar
D.   spe - ctac - ul - ar

41.   A.   rubber
B.   rub - ber
C.   rubb - er
D.   ru - bber

Read <u>all</u> answer choices before selecting one.

Directions: Read each sentence, and then choose the word that best fits in each blank.

The ___42___ went to the ___43___ in a taxi, but when he got there, he couldn't pay the ___44___.
A.   fare   B.   bare   C.   bear   D.   fair

Dinner ___45___ at ___46___ house is an event not to be ___47___.
A.   mist   B.   hour   C.   our   D.   missed

Our ___48___ went up to our ___49___ in the hotel to eat the ___50___ sticky-buns that the coach had bought for us.
A.   teem   B.   sweet   C.   team   D.   suite

The ___51___ on our vacation didn't ___52___ ___53___ much.
A.   whether   B.   vary   C.   weather   D.   very

Name: _____ Date: _____

Lesson Two: Word Analysis (cont.)

> **Directions:** Answer the following questions about the origin of each of the words below.

54. Which of these words came from an Arabic phrase that meant "commander at sea"?
    A.   captain   B.   admiral   C.   allied   D.   sailor

55. Which of these words came from Latin words meaning "the cultivation of land"?
    A.   agreement   B.   farming   C.   combine   D.   agriculture

56. Which of these words came from a French word meaning "a document with a wax seal on it"?
    A.   bill   B.   letter   C.   note   D.   paper

57. Which of these words came from an old French phrase meaning "the tooth of a lion"?
    A.   dandelion   B.   Lion King   C.   teeth   D.   sharp

58. Which of these words came from a Greek word for "new"?
    A.   modern   B.   recent   C.   neon   D.   novel

59. Which of these words came from an old German word that meant "to strike with the beak"?
    A.   peek   B.   peck   C.   peel   D.   peep

60. Which of these words came from two Hawaiian words: "jumping" and "flea"?
    A.   guitar   B.   banjo   C.   violin   D.   ukulele

Review

1. Be sure that you understand the directions.

2. Format changes <u>may</u> <u>not</u> signal a change in directions, so don't be fooled!

3. Look for key words in the directions ... like *root word*, for example.

4. If you aren't sure which answer is correct, then guess.

5. Read <u>all</u> answer choices before selecting one.

Name: _____ Date: _____

UNIT ONE: READING

Lesson Three: Comprehension

Directions: Read the paragraphs, and then choose the word that best fits the sentences.

Angel of the Battlefield

Clara Barton was born on Christmas Day in 1821 in Massachusetts. She was the youngest child of a farmer and state legislator who had fought in the Revolutionary War. She often sat at the feet of her father listening to his tales of that war. These stories made war very familiar to her.

Because she was well-spoken and well-read, Clara became a teacher at the age of 15. She taught in New Jersey where she managed to establish several free schools. When she first started teaching in New Jersey, the state charged tuition for attending the school; therefore, hardly any students attended. Barton offered to teach free if the state would do away with the tuition cost for students. The result was a huge rise in enrollment; her class went from 6 students to 600 students!

Clara's war service began with the Civil War in April 1861. When the Sixth Massachusetts Regiment arrived in Washington without any of its baggage, which had been lost along the route, she set about searching for replacements to supply the soldiers' needs. She tore up old sheets for towels and handkerchiefs and began cooking for the troops. After the Battle of Bull Run, she became aware of the severe shortages of supplies in the field, so she advertised for provisions in a newspaper. The response was overwhelming; the public sent in huge amounts. As a result, Clara established a distribution center.

In 1862, Clara Barton got government permission to accompany the sick and wounded soldiers home. She was named superintendent of nurses for the Army of the James in 1864. Barton showed courage, endurance, and resourcefulness on the battlefield and gave sympathetic aid to many.

Clara established the American branch of the Red Cross in 1881. From 1882 to 1904 she was president of the organization. Her commitment to the cause of helping others was unwavering. She was one of America's greatest heroines and humanitarians. She was a true patriot and philanthropist who, when she saw a need, gave every ounce of her strength and wit to address it. Her devotion to human welfare and her good works earned her the nickname "Angel of the Battlefield. "

Name: _____ Date: _____

Lesson Three: Comprehension (cont.)

1. The schools in New Jersey charged students _____.
   A. tuition
   B. enrollment
   C. superintendent
   D. resigned

2. The _____ of a school refers to the number of students who attend.
   A. tuition
   B. enrollment
   C. superintendent
   D. resigned

3. Barton showed great _____ on the battlefield.
   A. endurance
   B. courage
   C. resourcefulness
   D. commitment

4. In acquiring supplies for the needy soldiers, Clara Barton showed amazing _____.
   A. endurance
   B. courage
   C. resourcefulness
   D. commitment

5. A _____ is a person, like Clara Barton, who loves, supports, and defends her country.
   A. heroine
   B. humanitarian
   C. patriot
   D. philanthropist

6. Clara Barton, a _____, helped many people by making generous gifts of time, money, and much-needed supplies.
   A. heroine
   B. humanitarian
   C. patriot
   D. philanthropist

Name: _____ Date: _____

Lesson Three: Comprehension (cont.)

Directions: Answer the following questions using the paragraphs about Clara Barton.

7. Why did Barton give up her teaching salary in New Jersey?
   A.   She didn't need it anymore.
   B.   So students could attend school free.
   C.   She wanted the town officials to buy books.
   D.   She was forced to by the government.

8. Clara Barton held of all these jobs except that of
   A.   teacher.
   B.   nurse.
   C.   school administrator.
   D.   government administrator.

9. Why was Clara Barton so interested in things military?
   A.   She wanted to be a boy and do boy things.
   B.   She had a soft heart and felt sorry for the soldiers.
   C.   She was well-read on the subject.
   D.   Her father had told her war stories when she was young.

10. How old was Miss Barton when she began teaching?
    A.   14
    B.   15
    C.   16
    D.   18

11. Clara Barton established which organization in America?
    A.   The Red Cross
    B.   The Girl Scouts
    C.   The Visiting Nurse Association
    D.   The Salvation Army

12. Which of these is <u>not</u> an opinion?
    A.   Clara Barton is one of America's greatest heroines.
    B.   Clara showed courage and endurance on the battlefield.
    C.   Clara became a teacher in New Jersey.
    D.   Barton cared very much for the suffering of others.

Name: _____ Date: _____

Lesson Three: Comprehension (cont.)

Directions: Read the passage about The First Ladies, and then answer questions 13–17.

The First Ladies

Martha Washington, the wife of the first President of the United States, became the first, first lady when she took up residence in the President's House in New York City in 1789. She was the first in a long history to experience the fascination the American people have for the first lady. Since Martha's time, the interest of the American people in the wife of their president has grown continually stronger and more warmhearted.

From the moment her husband becomes president, a first lady's life changes. She becomes a public figure—a celebrity of sorts whose face is seen thousands of times in magazines, in newspapers, and on televisions across America and the world. She becomes the country's official hostess, welcoming rulers of many nations who come to the White House. She meets and greets people from all walks of life, occupations, and parts of the world and welcomes them on behalf of the American people. As a public figure, her personal life must take second place to her responsibilities as first lady.

Perhaps her biggest job is running the president's official house, the White House. There are 132 rooms in the White House and a large staff of household employees. It is the first lady's job to see that the White House staff does its work well. Since the White House is the only American house that many important visitors see, it is the first lady's job to make sure that everything is well-run and that the White House is a pleasant place to visit.

Duties of the first lady have continually grown more demanding as the United States has grown in importance among the nations of the world. Recent first ladies have been expected to entertain people whose language and customs are completely different from those of the United States and to travel to foreign countries as an "unofficial" ambassador of our country. In addition, millions of people, tourists, famous diplomats, and political and social figures pass through the White House each year.

There is little privacy for the first lady and her family. Almost everything she and other members of her family do becomes the subject of newspaper and magazine stories. Often their activities are reported on national and worldwide news. This is one aspect of the life of a first lady that many first ladies dislike. It is especially difficult for those first ladies who have tried to raise their children in the White House.

Many first ladies, despite all of their difficult and numerous household duties, have played important roles in their husbands' careers and in the life of the nation. It remains to be seen what role and responsibilities a "first man" will have when a married woman is elected to the White House.

Lesson Three: Comprehension (cont.)

13. Who was the first, first lady of the United States?
    A.   Martha Washington
    B.   Abigail Adams
    C.   Dolley Madison
    D.   Laura Bush

14. All but which one of these are duties of the first lady?
    A.   to welcome people to the White House
    B.   to entertain political figures and diplomats
    C.   to clean the White House
    D.   to travel with the president

15. How many rooms does the White House have?
    A.   150 rooms
    B.   132 rooms
    C.   32 rooms
    D.   100 rooms

16. Which of these is a responsibility most first ladies dislike?
    A.   meeting and greeting people
    B.   campaigning with and for their husbands
    C.   being in the public eye
    D.   running the White House

17. Why is it important that the first lady see that the White House is well-run and maintained?
    A.   It is a model of home life in America.
    B.   The White House is a national treasure.
    C.   As a wife, it is her duty to take care of the home.
    D.   It is the only American home many important world visitors see.

Name: _____ Date: _____

Lesson Three: Comprehension (cont.)

> **Directions:** Read the recipe, and then answer the questions.

YUMMY BROWNIES

1 box brownie mix
1/2 cup egg substitute
1 tsp. vanilla extract
1/8 tsp. nutmeg
Spray oil

1/3 cup water
1/3 cup chocolate syrup
1/8 tsp. cinnamon
1 cup nut pieces, optional

Get a grown-up to preheat your oven to 350 degrees.
Spray the bottom of an 8″ x 8″ pan.
In a big bowl, mix the brownie stuff and the cinnamon and nutmeg.
Make a hole in the mix and put in the wet stuff.
Stir about 50 times or until there are no more lumps.
Add some nuts if you want to.
Have a grown-up help you pour it all into a pan.
Bake for about 28 to 30 minutes or until you can poke it with a toothpick in the middle and it comes out cakey. Don't cook it too long; the middle may still look a little wet, but it's good. Make sure you let the pan get cold before you cut the brownies.

---

18. To make these brownies, what is the first thing to do?
    A. Preheat the oven.
    B. Mix the brownie mix.
    C. Gather the ingredients.
    D. Bake for 28–30 minutes.

19. What is the second thing to do?
    A. Preheat the oven.
    B. Mix the brownie mix.
    C. Gather the ingredients.
    D. Bake for 28–30 minutes.

20. What is the <u>last</u> thing you do when baking brownies?
    A. Pour the mix in the pan.
    B. Bake for 28–30 minutes.
    C. Cool and cut the brownies.
    D. Eat the brownies.

21. How hot do you make your oven when baking these brownies?
    A. 300°   B. 325°   C. 350°   D. 375°

22. How do you know when the brownies are done?
    A. when the brownies have baked for 30 minutes
    B. when a toothpick poked in the middle comes out cakey
    C. when they look done to you
    D. when the timer goes off

Name: _____ Date: _____

Lesson Three: Comprehension (cont.)

23. What spices are in this recipe?
    A. salt and pepper
    B. allspice
    C. cinnamon and nutmeg
    D. thyme and sage

Directions: Read the poems, and then answer the questions.

Knitted Things

There was a witch who knitted things:
Elephants and playground swings.
She knitted rain,
She knitted night,
But nothing really came out right.
The elephants had just one tusk
And night looked more
Like dawn or dusk.
The rain was snow
And when she tried
To knit an egg
It came out fried.
She knitted birds
With buttonholes
And twenty rubber butter rolls.
She knitted blue angora trees.
She purl stitched countless purple fleas.
She knitted a palace in need of a darn.
She knitted a battle and ran out of yarn.
She drew out a strand
Of her gleaming, green hair
And knitted a lawn
Till she just wasn't there.

— By Karla Kuskin

Poetry is the expression of ideas or feelings put into words.

The Yak

There was a most odious Yak
Who took only toads on his Back;
If you asked for a Ride,
He would act very Snide,
And go humping off, yicketty-yak.

— By Theodore Roethke

My Papa's Waltz

The whisky on your breath
Could make a small boy dizzy;
but I hung on like death:
Such waltzing was not easy.

We romped until the pan
Slid from the kitchen shelf;
My mother's countenance
Could not unfrown itself.

The hand that held my wrist
Was battered on one knuckle;
At every step you missed
My right ear scraped a buckle.

You beat time on my head
With a palm caked hard by dirt,
Then waltzed me off to bed
Still clinging to your shirt.

— By Theodore Roethke

18

Name: _____ Date: _____

Lesson Three: Comprehension (cont.)

24. "Knitted Things" is about
    A. a wicked witch.
    B. a mixed-up witch.
    C. a witch who could not knit very well.
    D. a witch with green hair.

25. Which statement is true about "Knitted Things"?
    A. The author's purpose was to entertain the reader.
    B. The author didn't use rhyme.
    C. All lines have the same number of syllables.
    D. This poem is a series of couplets.

26. Which of these is an example of alliteration in the poem, "Knitted Things"?
    A. countless purple fleas
    B. She knitted a battle and ran out of yarn.
    C. But nothing came out right
    D. Of her gleaming, green hair

27. "My Papa's Waltz" is about
    A. a small girl dancing with her father.
    B. a small boy dancing with his beloved father.
    C. a farmer and his wife waltzing in the kitchen.
    D. a father dancing for his family.

28. What line in the poem tells you that the narrator is small?
    A. My right ear scraped a buckle.
    B. You beat time on my head
    C. Then waltzed me off to bed
    D. Still clinging to your shirt

29. What is the setting for "My Papa's Waltz"?
    A. a wedding
    B. a barn
    C. a kitchen
    D. a bedroom

Look for the BEST answer. More than one answer may be *true*, but which one answers the question?

30. The lines, "My mother's countenance
    Could not unfrown itself" mean
    A. My mother could not stop laughing.
    B. My mother would not smile.
    C. My mother's face was one big thundercloud.
    D. My mother would not stop frowning.

Name: _____ Date: _____

Lesson Three: Comprehension (cont.)

31. "The Yak" is an example of a
    A. rhyme.
    B. limerick.
    C. lyric
    D. ballad.

32. What is another word or phrase for *odious* in line 1 of "The Yak"?
    A. most unpleasant
    B. delightful
    C. stinky
    D. beautiful

33. What does it mean, in line 4 of "The Yak," "He would act very Snide"?
    A. He would act as if he didn't know.
    B. He acted in an insulting manner.
    C. He acted like you weren't even there.
    D. He acted superior to people.

34. To whom does "he" refer in line 4 of "The Yak"?
    A. the witch
    B. the boy
    C. the yak
    D. the man

35. Which of these is an example of a figure of speech?
    A. He must be eight feet tall.
    B. one bright day, in the middle of the night
    C. It's raining cats and dogs.
    D. a jumbo shrimp

36. Which is an example of an oxymoron?
    A. He must be eight feet tall.
    B. One bright day, in the middle of the night.
    C. It's raining cats and dogs.
    D. a jumbo shrimp

37. Which of these is an example of a metaphor?
    A. He is a giant teddy bear!
    B. The wind whispered through the night.
    C. He wasn't unhappy about winning the bet.
    D. Tom is barking up the wrong tree.

If you aren't sure which answer is correct and you are running out of time, then guess!

Name: _____ Date: _____

Lesson Three: Comprehension (cont.)

38. Which of these is an example of personification?
    A.   He is a giant teddy bear!
    B.   The wind whispered through the night.
    C.   He wasn't unhappy about winning the bet.
    D.   Tom is barking up the wrong tree.

39. What is meant by the <u>plot</u> of a story?
    A.   the form, rhythm, and rhyme of the story
    B.   the storyline or events that happen in a story
    C.   the lesson that a story teaches
    D.   the way a story is narrated

40. The story about Clara Barton is told from which point of view?
    A.   the first-person point of view
    B.   the third-person point of view
    C.   both the first and third person points of view
    D.   neither the first nor the third person point of view

---

Directions: Read the play carefully, and then answer the questions.

The Brahman and the Tiger

(*The Brahman, a very wise and kindly man, is walking along a road in India when he comes upon a fierce tiger in a large iron cage. The road leads to a village at the edge of the jungle.*)

TIGER: Brother Brahman, Brother Brahman, let me out of this cage for one minute, or I shall die of thirst. I want only to get a drink of water.

BRAHMAN: No, I will not. The villagers caught you and locked you up because you had been eating men, and if I let you out of the cage, you will eat me.

TIGER: I promise I will not. I will never be so mean. Only let me out, that I may drink some water and return to the jungle. I shall soon die of thirst.

(*The Brahman is grieved to see the tiger so thirsty and unlocks the cage door.*)

TIGER: (*Jumping out*) Ha! Ha! I am out. Now I shall kill you first and eat you, and then drink the water.

BRAHMAN: Wait a bit. Do not be in such a hurry to kill me. Let us first ask the opinion of six. If all of them say that you are being just and fair, then I am willing to die.

Name: _____ Date: _____

Lesson Three: Comprehension (cont.)

TIGER: Very well. It shall be as you say. We will ask the opinion of six.

(*The tiger and the Brahman walk along until they come to a fig tree.*)

BRAHMAN: Fig Tree, Fig Tree, hear and give judgment.

FIG TREE: On what must I give judgment?

BRAHMAN: This tiger begged me to let him out of his cage to get a drink of water. He promised not to hurt me if I did so. Now that I have let him out, he wishes to eat me. Is it just that he should do so, or not?

FIG TREE: I give cool shade from the hot sun to all who come this way. When they have rested, they cut and break my branches. Let the tiger eat the man.

TIGER: Ha! Ha! I shall eat you now.

BRAHMAN: No, Tiger, you must not kill me yet, for you promised that we should first hear the judgment of six. Come a little farther.

TIGER: Very well.

(*They go on their way, and after a little while they meet a camel.*)

41. What was the Brahman seeking?
    A. to go on alone in peace
    B. a fair opinion on the matter
    C. to soar higher and higher
    D. to become more clever than the tiger

42. Why did the fig tree decide against the Brahman?
    A. because the fig tree and the tiger belonged, and the Brahman didn't
    B. because the fig tree liked the tiger more than the Brahman
    C. because the fig tree had been abused by man so he decided against him
    D. because the fig tree was afraid of the tiger

43. How did the tiger get in the cage to begin with?
    A. The Brahman put him in.
    B. The fig tree put him in.
    C. The villagers put him in.
    D. The camel put him in.

A play is a story written to be acted out in front of an audience.

Name: _____ Date: _____

Lesson Three: Comprehension (cont.)

44. What does it mean in the story when it says, "The Brahman is <u>grieved</u> ..."?
    A. The Brahman felt great fear.
    B. The Brahman felt bad for getting tricked.
    C. The Brahman was very curious.
    D. The Brahman was sad to see the thirsty tiger.

Directions: Read the sentences carefully, and then choose the correct order of events in the play.

---

1. The tiger asked the Brahman to do something.
2. The Brahman and the tiger met a camel.
3. The Brahman asked the opinion of fig tree.
4. The fig tree decided in favor of the tiger.

45. A. 1, 2, 3, 4
    B. 3, 2, 4, 1
    C. 2, 3, 4, 1
    D. 1, 3, 4, 2

Directions: Read this article, and then answer the questions.

---

[1]Animals can protect themselves in many ways. [2]Some animals are born with weapons. [3]Several, like goats, the wildebeest, and the kudu, have horns. [4]Others, like the members of the cat family, have claws. [5]Baboons, tigers, and bears have sharp, deadly teeth. [6]The teeth of elephants and wild boars are powerful tusks.

46. Which sentence tells the main idea of the paragraph?
    A. sentence 1
    B. sentence 2
    C. sentence 4
    D. sentence 6

47. Animals use all but which one for fighting?
    A. horns
    B. claw
    C. spit
    D. teeth

Name: _____ Date: _____

Lesson Three: Comprehension (cont.)

> [1]The deer and antelope can run up to forty-five miles per hour. [2]Rabbits can take long zigzag jumps. [3]Birds take to the wing. [4]Others, like the chipmunks, rats, and woodchucks, run into their burrows where the larger enemies cannot follow. [5]These animals depend on flight to escape their enemies.

48. Which sentence tells the main idea of this paragraph?
    A.   sentence 1
    B.   sentence 3
    C.   sentence 5
    D.   sentence 4

49. Some animals flee from their enemies in all but which way?
    A.   running
    B.   hopping
    C.   flying
    D.   jumping

> [1]Many animals are protected by their natural coloring. [2]Some tiny sea animals are almost transparent. [3]Several furred animals, such as some rabbits, martens, and ermine are brown in the summer, but change to white in the winter when there is snow on the ground.

50. What would be a good title for the above two paragraphs?
    A.   How Animals Protect Themselves
    B.   Hiding in Plain Sight
    C.   Animals with Weapons
    D.   Animals Can Fight

> Read back over your test to be sure you answered all of the questions.

Name: _____ Date: _____

Lesson Three: Comprehension (cont.)

Review

1. When testing reading comprehension, you are asked to read for details and meaning.

2. When uncertain, look back in the passage for the information.

3. Use context clues to figure out words or ideas you don't understand.

4. Sequence of events is important for comprehension.

5. Watch out for negatives like <u>not</u> or <u>the one that isn't correct</u>. Sometimes you are looking for the *wrong* answer rather than the right one.

6. Poetry is the expression of ideas or feelings put into words.

7. Look for the BEST answer. More than one may be true, but which one answers the question?

8. If you aren't sure which answer is correct, then guess!

9. A play is a story written to be acted out in front of an audience.

10. Read back over your test to be sure you answered all of the questions.

Helpful Language Strategies

Test Tips

1. The most important test tip is to be <u>confident</u>. You are not supposed to know <u>all</u> of the answers, just most of them.
2. Read all maps, charts, graphs, and diagrams carefully.
3. Decide what you think the answer is before reading the choices. Then look and see if your answer is there.
4. Read all answer choices before answering the question.
5. Choose your answers carefully. More than one answer may *seem* correct.
6. Eliminate those choices you know are wrong or don't make sense.
7. Don't look ahead to another question until you finish the one you are working on.
8. Make sure you fill in the right number and letter on your answer sheet.
9. Think twice before you change an answer; it is usually not a good idea to change an answer, as your first guess is usually the correct one.
10. If you *have* to change an answer, be sure you erase your mistake completely.
11. Remember, all you can do is your personal best!

Language Strategies

★ Language tests usually include questions about spelling, grammar, punctuation, and capitalization.

★ Standard English is the kind of language you read in books and hear on the news.

★ When in doubt, say the answer choices quietly to yourself. Which one *sounds* correct?

★ Use context clues to figure out tough questions.

★ The purpose of punctuation is to signal meaning to the reader.

★ If you are not sure of the spelling, try writing the word out on scrap paper. Which word *looks* right?

★ When sentences are combined, make sure the meaning of the sentence is not changed.

Name: _____   Date: _____

UNIT TWO: LANGUAGE

Lesson One: Mechanics

Search and Rescue Dogs

[1]Shortly after the disaster of the Twin Towers, search and rescue dogs and their handlers were searching through the dust and debris for victims, alive and dead. [2]Wherever and whenever disaster strikes, the search and rescue dogs and they're handlers are their. [3]Whenever an earthquake rumbles, an avalanche roars, a building collapses, a tornado rips through a Midwestern town, a hurricane brings destruction to the Gulf Coast or eastern seaboard, or a bomb reduces a federal building to rubble, the search and rescue dogs are on the scene.

[4]Search and rescue dogs are the hard-working hero's of disaster re_____. [5]With a sense of smell more powerful than a human's and the ability to probe nooks and crannies that humans cannot penetrate, these dogs save lives and bring comfort to the families whose friends and relatives are caught in the tragedies.

[6]Favorite breeds for rescue work are German Shepherds Belgian Malinois and Golden Retrievers. [7]Any medium-to-large breed or mix works just as well, however. [8]A Search and Rescue dog must enjoy tracking and be able to concentrate on following a scent. [9]Rescue dogs must be able to focus on the task at hand—to find the scent no matter where it leads or how much it is intermingled with other odors.

---

1. How many two-syllable words are there in sentence 1?
   A. 8   B. 9   C. 10   D. 15

2. Which of these are the correct spellings (sentence 2)?
   A. there handlers are their
   B. they're handlers are there
   C. their handlers are they're
   D. their handlers are there

> Language tests usually include questions about spelling, grammar, punctuation, and capitalization.

3. Which is correct for this phrase in sentence 3?
   A. a midwestern town
   B. a Midwestern Town
   C. a Midwestern town
   D. a midwestern Town

Name: _____ Date: _____

Lesson One: Mechanics (cont.)

4. In sentence 4, what is the correct spelling of the word with the blank?
   - A. releef
   - B. relief
   - C. releif
   - D. releaf

5. Which is the correct punctuation in sentence 6?
   - A. German Shepherds, Belgian Malinois, and Golden Retrievers.
   - B. German Shepherds, Belgian Malinois, and, Golden Retrievers.
   - C. German Shepherds Belgian Malinois, and, Golden Retrievers.
   - D. German Shepherds, Belgian Malinois, and Golden Retrievers

6. What is the correct spelling (sentence 4)?
   - A. heros
   - B. heroes
   - C. hero's
   - D. heroes'

7. What does the word <u>intermingled</u> (sentence 8) mean?
   - A. to interfere
   - B. to become an intermediary
   - C. to get between
   - D. to become mixed together

8. What are "nooks and crannies" (sentence 5)?
   - A. spaces under snow
   - B. windows and doors
   - C. very small spaces
   - D. mud and sludge

9. Which of these is the correct way to write search and rescue dogs (sentence 8)?
   - A. search and Rescue Dog
   - B. Search and Rescue dog
   - C. Search and Rescue Dog
   - D. search and rescue dog

10. All but which one are synonyms for the word *scent* in sentence 8?
    - A. taste
    - B. aroma
    - C. odor
    - D. smell

Eliminate choices that you know are wrong or that don't make sense.

Name: _____   Date: _____

Lesson One: Mechanics (cont.)

> **Directions:** Read each sentence, and then choose the correct way to capitalize the word or group of words that go in the blank.

11. My favorite book is _____11_____.
    A.   Harry Potter And The goblet Of fire
    B.   Harry Potter and the Goblet of Fire
    C.   Harry Potter and the goblet of fire
    D.   harry potter and the goblet of fire

> "Because ___12___ is ___13___, we don't have school", ___14___ Garcia reminded us.

12. A.   monday
    B.   Monday
    C.   Mon
    D.   mon.

13. A.   Lincoln's Birthday
    B.   lincoln's Birthday
    C.   Lincoln's birthday
    D.   lincoln's birthday

14. A.   mrs.
    B.   mrs
    C.   Mrs.
    D.   Mrs

Be sure you fill in the correct number and letter on your answer sheet.

> ___15___ favorite poem is ___16___ ___17___ by ___18___.

15. A.   my   B.   mine
    C.   My   D.   Mine

16. A.   Showdown at   B.   "showdown at
    C.   Show Down At   D.   "Showdown at

17. A.   pangaea creek,"   B.   Pangaea Creek"
    C.   Pangaea Creek,"   D.   Pangaea creek,

18. A.   michael R Evans   B.   Michael R. Evans
    C.   Michael r Evans   D.   Michael R. evans

Name: _____ Date: _____

Lesson One: Mechanics (cont.)

Directions: Choose the word that is misspelled. If there are no errors, choose D.

19. A. thret
    B. thousand
    C. thunder
    D. no mistakes

20. A. service
    B. citisen
    C. clumsy
    D. no mistakes

21. A. understood
    B. shampoo
    C. jewels
    D. no mistakes

22. A. manage
    B. firnachur
    C. capture
    D. no mistakes

23. A. turkey
    B. worship
    C. werst
    D. no mistakes

24. A. swimmer
    B. jogger
    C. collar
    D. no mistakes

25. A. accidentally
    B. increase
    C. enormus
    D. no mistakes

26. A. absent
    B. absence
    C. absorb
    D. no mistakes

27. A. visor
    B. voyce
    C. villain
    D. no mistakes

28. A. recieve
    B. recess
    C. restaurant
    D. no mistakes

When in doubt, try writing the word out on a piece of scrap paper. How does it look?

Directions: Choose the word that correctly completes the sentence.

29. Where did I _____ my mittens?
    A. left
    C. leave
    B. leved
    D. let

30. Our cat _____ very quickly not to sit on the stove.
    A. taught
    C. learn
    B. teached
    D. learned

Name: _____ Date: _____

Lesson One: Mechanics (cont.)

31. Sheena has _____ to the store.
    A. went   B. gone
    C. go   D. going

32. The _____ of people who cared was amazing!
    A. number   B. amount
    C. size   D. sum

33. _____ did you meet at the mall?
    A. Who   B. Whom
    C. Whose   D. Who's

34. To _____ was the letter addressed?
    A. who   B. whom
    C. whose   D. who's

35. _____ idea did the teacher choose?
    A. Who   B. Whom
    C. Whose   D. Who's

> Standard English or "correct language" is the kind you read in books and hear on the news.

Review

1. Language tests usually include questions about spelling, grammar, punctuation, and capitalization.

2. Eliminate choices you know are wrong or don't make sense.

3. Be sure you fill in the correct number and letter on your answer sheet.

4. When in doubt, try writing the word out on a piece of scrap paper. Which *looks* right?

5. Remember, Standard English or "correct language" is the kind of language you read in books and hear on the news.

Name: _____   Date: _____

UNIT TWO: LANGUAGE

Lesson Two: Expression

Directions: Read the story, and then answer the questions.

¹One day, two friends were walking down one of the busiest streets in the city. ²Like all big cities, there was a lot of noise ... cars were honking their horns, feet were shuffling along, people were talking, sirens were wailing. ³Suddenly, one of the friends, Nathaniel, said that he heard a cricket chirp.

"No way," said his friend, Kathryn. ⁵"You couldn't possibly hear a cricket chirp in all of this noise. ⁶You must be imagining it. ⁷Besides, there are no crickets in the city."

⁸Nathaniel said, "I really hear a cricket, honest. ⁹I'll show you." ¹⁰He took Kathryn across the street to a big cement planter with a tree in it. ¹⁰There beneath the leaves was the cricket! ¹²"That is amazing," Kathryn said, "You must have superhuman hearing. ¹³What's your secret?"

¹⁴"My hearing is the same as yours," he said. "There's no secret—watch, I'll show you." ¹⁵He reached in his pocket and pulled out a handful of loose change and threw it on the sidewalk. ¹⁶Amid all the noises of the city, every head within twenty feet turned to see where the sound of money was coming from.

¹⁷"See," he said, "it's all a matter of what you're listening for."

Decide what you think the answer is before reading the choices. Then compare the answer choices.

Name: _____ Date: _____

Lesson Two: Expression (cont.)

1. What is the main idea of this story?
   A. Crickets don't live in cities.
   B. Listen to your friends.
   C. Be aware of your surroundings.
   D. Hold on to your money.

2. Where was the cricket found?
   A. across the street in a planter
   B. in the man's imagination
   C. across the street in an empty building
   D. in the man's pocket

3. The pronoun *he* is in the third sentence. To whom does *he* refer?
   A. cricket
   B. Kathryn
   C. noise
   D. Nathaniel

4. What was the secret to Nathaniel's hearing?
   A. He had superhuman ability to hear.
   B. No secret, he just paid attention.
   C. Nathaniel refused to tell his secret.
   D. He had an operation on his ears.

5. Which is the best way to combine sentences 1 and 2 without changing the meaning?
   A. Nathaniel and Kathryn, amid all the noise, were walking down the street of the city.
   B. The noisy city was where Nathaniel and Kathryn were walking.
   C. Two friends were walking down one of the busiest streets in the city and, like all big cities, there was a lot of noise.
   D. There was a lot of noise in the city as two friends walked down the street.

Directions: Choose the subject of each sentence.

---

6. <u>Buddy Holly</u> was <u>one</u> of the <u>greatest</u> rock 'n' roll <u>songwriters</u>.
       A   B   C   D

7. Between <u>1957 and 1959,</u> <u>he</u> had <u>seven</u> hit <u>singles</u>.
                A   B   C   D

8. Sometimes <u>Holly</u> sang with his <u>band</u>, while at other <u>times</u> he performed <u>solo</u>.
         A   B   C   D

Name: _____   Date: _____

Lesson Two: Expression (cont.)

9.   <u>Songs</u> like *Peggy Sue* became <u>instant</u> <u>classics</u>.
        A   B   C   D

10.   When <u>Buddy Holly</u> died in a <u>plane</u> <u>crash</u>, the <u>world</u> was shocked.
                    A   B   C   D

Directions: Choose the predicate in each sentence.

---

11.   In <u>1992</u>, <u>Kristi Yamaguchi</u> <u>skated</u> in the Olympics <u>for</u> a gold medal.
           A   B   C   D

12.   <u>Yamaguchi</u> <u>began</u> her <u>skating</u> <u>career</u> as a partner in pairs skating.
           A   B   C   D

13.   At the age of <u>six</u>, <u>she</u> <u>started</u> <u>skating</u>.
                        A   B   C   D

14.   <u>Yamaguchi</u> <u>practiced</u> <u>skating</u> several <u>hours</u> a day.
           A   B   C   D

15.   In 1990, <u>Yamaguchi</u> <u>decided</u> to <u>change</u> from pairs <u>skating</u> to singles skating.
                    A   B   C   D

Directions: For questions 16 and 17, read the paragraph and choose the best topic sentence.

_____. A submarine floats on the surface of the water when its tanks are full of air. If water is pumped into the tanks, the submarine begins to sink. To come back to the surface of the water, the tanks are again pumped full of air, which forces the water out.

16.   A.   Submarines are really interesting.
        B.   Have you ever wondered about submarines?
        C.   We got to ride in a yellow submarine.
        D.   Submarines are underwater boats.

Name: _____ Date: _____

Lesson Two: Expression (cont.)

_____. The northern part of the country is in the Himalayan mountains. Most of the people live in the valleys where it is very fertile. They raise sheep and goats and yaks. Kathmandu is the capital of Nepal. Visitors from all over the world come to Nepal to climb the world's highest mountain, Mount Everest.

17. A. The country of Nepal is between India and Tibet.
    B. I chose Nepal as my country to write about.
    C. Nepal is a small Asian country.
    D. I have never been to Nepal, but I would like to visit.

Directions: Choose the sentence that best supports each of the topic sentences.

18. What is a Przewalski?
    A. Przewalskis are smaller than regular horses. These mini-horses have stubby bodies, large heads, thick necks, and a dark stripe down their backs.
    B. Przewalskis are horses. I love horses. I go riding every day after school. Horses are a lot of work, but I still want to get one.
    C. Today, there are about 1,200 Przewalski horses living in zoos. These captured horses are being gradually released into their native habitats.
    D. These horses are part of Mongolian culture. They live on the border between Mongolia and China.

19. Who is your hero?
    A. A superhero has a transformed body. He or she has extraordinary powers or talents. A superhero fights extremely dangerous villains.
    B. Anne Frank was a young Jewish girl who hid from the Nazis during World War II. She kept a secret diary that was published after her death.
    C. My mom is my hero. She is very busy both at work as a teacher and at home. She cares a lot for her students and loves us kids.
    D. There are no more heroes in the world today. Every time I turn on the television, another sports hero has done something bad.

Name: _____ Date: _____

Lesson Two: Expression (cont.)

Directions: Read the following sentences, noting the underlined pronoun. Choose the word to which the pronoun refers.

20. Corn, peas, and potatoes are my favorite vegetables. I could eat <u>them</u> for every meal.
    A.   potatoes
    B.   vegetables
    C.   corn, peas, and potatoes
    D.   meal

21. Mrs. Abbas needs a babysitter for <u>her</u> daughter tonight.
    A.   Mrs. Abbas
    B.   babysitter
    C.   daughter
    D.   tonight

22. After Marala's umbrella blew inside out, <u>it</u> didn't work any more.
    A.   Marala
    B.   umbrella
    C.   blew
    D.   out

23. John and Jane wrote the book. They also illustrated <u>it</u>.
    A.   John
    B.   John and Jane
    C.   They
    D.   book

24. My cousin drove the car by <u>himself</u>.
    A.   My
    B.   cousin
    C.   car
    D.   drove

25. Your truck has a bed liner like the one in <u>mine</u>.
    A.   Your
    B.   truck
    C.   bed liner
    D.   like

Name: _____ Date: _____

UNIT TWO: LANGUAGE

Lesson Three: Information Skills

Directions: Examine the map in Figure 1 carefully, and then answer the questions.

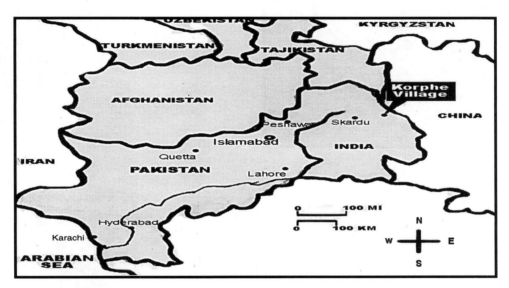

Figure 1

1. All of these countries border Afghanistan except
    A. Turkmenistan.
    B. Uzbekistan.
    C. Kyrgyzstan.
    D. Pakistan.

2. Islamabad is _____ of Karachi.
    A. Northeast
    B. Northwest
    C. Southeast
    D. Southwest

Eliminate those choices you know are wrong or that don't make sense.

3. How long is the border between Iran and Pakistan?
    A. about 100 miles
    B. about 200 miles
    C. about 400 miles
    D. more than 500 miles

Name: _____ Date: _____

Lesson Three: Information Skills (cont.)

Directions: Examine the diagram in Figure 2, and then answer the questions.

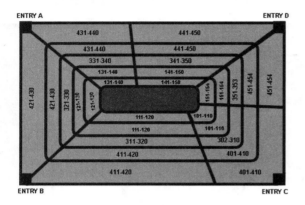

It is usually not a good idea to change your answer, as your first guess is usually the correct one.

Figure 2

4. Your tickets for the big concert are numbered 143 and 144. Which entrance is closest to your seats?
   A. Entry A
   B. Entry B
   C. Entry C
   D. Entry D

5. Which of these would be the best tickets for a football game in this dome?
   A. 421, 422
   B. 113, 114
   C. 124, 125
   D. 302, 303

Directions: Examine the signs in Figure 3, and then answer the questions.

Figure 3

Name: _____   Date: _____

Lesson Three: Information Skills (cont.)

6. Which of these is a bike route sign?
    A. A   B. B   C. C   D. D

7. Which sign indicates a school crossing?
    A. A   B. B   C. C   D. D

8. Which sign indicates an intersection up ahead?
    A. A   B. B   C. C   D. D

9. If you needed information about the country of Malawi, in which of these books would you look?
    A. dictionary
    B. atlas
    C. encyclopedia
    D. thesaurus

If you **must** change an answer, be sure to erase your mistake carefully.

10. If you wanted to view a map of Malawi, in which of these would you look?
    A. dictionary
    B. atlas
    C. encyclopedia
    D. thesaurus

Directions: Read the chart of the Dewey Decimal Classification in Figure 4, and then answer the questions.

Figure 4

000	**Computers, Information, General Reference**
100	**Philosophy and Psychology**
200	**Religion**
300	**Social Science**
400	**Language**
500	**Science**
600	**Technology**
700	**Arts and Recreation**
800	**Literature**
900	**History and Geography**

Name: _____　　Date: _____

Lesson Three: Information Skills (cont.)

11. Where in the library would you go for more information on where Malawi is located?
    A.　200 section
    B.　300 section
    C.　500 section
    D.　900 section

12. If you wanted more information on Chickewa, the native language of Malawi, in which section would you look?
    A.　400 section
    B.　500 section
    C.　700 section
    D.　800 section

> **Directions:** Examine the title page in Figure 5, and then answer the questions.

13. Who wrote the book?
    A.　Harcourt Brace
    B.　Kathryn Hewitt
    C.　Brace Jovanovich
    D.　Kathleen Krull

14. Who illustrated the book?
    A.　Harcourt Brace
    B.　Kathryn Hewitt
    C.　Brace Jovanovich
    D.　Kathleen Krull

15. Where was the book published?
    A.　Los Angeles
    B.　Buffalo
    C.　San Diego
    D.　Madrid

16. What is the subtitle of this book?
    A.　Lives of the Musicians
    B.　Good Times, Bad Times
    C.　What the Neighbors Thought
    D.　Harcourt Brace Jovanovich

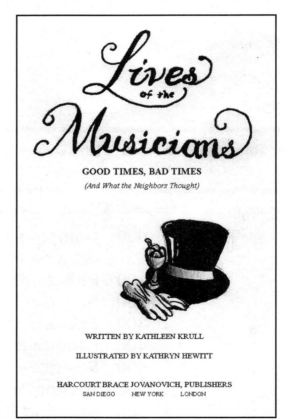

Figure 5

Name: _____ Date: _____

Lesson Three: Information Skills (cont.)

17. If you wanted to know if Mozart is in this book, where in the book would you look to find out?
    A.   Table of Contents
    B.   Footnotes
    C.   Thumb through the book
    D.   Title page

18. You are curious about why this book was written. Where in the book would you look?
    A.   Title page
    B.   Copyright page
    C.   Dedication
    D.   Introduction

Don't look ahead to another question until you complete the one you are working on.

Choose your answers carefully. More than one answer may <u>seem</u> correct.

Directions: Examine Figure 6, an entry from a thesaurus, and then answer the questions.

big, enormous, great, huge, large ■ All of these adjectives can mean "above the average in size."
Factory outlet stores usually offer **big** *discounts.*
A computer can store an **enormous** *amount of information.*
A **great** *number of people attended the concert.*
I took a **huge** *helping of mashed potatoes.*
Los Angeles is a **large** *city.*
Antonyms: little, small

Figure 6

Name: _____ Date: _____

Lesson Three: Information Skills (cont.)

19. Which is the entry word?
    A. big
    B. enormous
    C. great
    D. antonyms

20. Which of these words is the opposite of *big*?
    A. great
    B. huge
    C. large
    D. small

Directions: Read the entry below from a library card catalog, and then answer the questions.

MATERIAL:	Book
AUTHOR:	Dahl, Roald
ILLUSTRATOR:	Blake, Quentin
TITLE:	*James and the Giant Peach*
PUBLICATION:	New York: Puffin Books, 2001
SUBJECT HEADINGS:	fairy tales
DESCRIPTION:	146 p.: ill; 20 cm.
NOTES:	A young boy escapes from two wicked aunts and embarks on a journey.

Figure 7

21. Who wrote the book?
    A. Puffin Books
    B. Quentin Blake
    C. Roald Dahl
    D. Steven Kellogg

22. How many pages are in the book?
    A. 20
    B. 146
    C. 2,001
    D. 150

Remember, all you can do is your personal best!

Lesson Three: Information Skills (cont.)

23. Who published the book?
    A. New York Books
    B. Roald Dahl
    C. Fairy Tales
    D. Puffin Books

24. Who illustrated the book?
    A. Quentin Blake
    B. Puffin Books
    C. Roald Dahl
    D. Kathryn Hewitt

25. In Figure 8, which number indicates the hard drive?
    A. 3   B. 2
    C. 4   D. 1

26. What is a modem?
    A. a device that links a computer to other computers through telephone lines
    B. a device that scans a picture and prints it
    C. a device that lets you explore the World Wide Web
    D. a device that acts as the brain of the computer

27. In the drawing (Figure 8), on which device would a cursor appear?
    A. 3   C. 4
    B. 6   D. 2

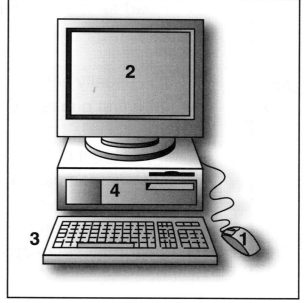

Figure 8

28. What does a scanner do?
    A. It copies something just like a copy machine.
    B. It "takes a picture" and turns it into a computer image.
    C. It examines all the possibilities for computer usage.
    D. It sends messages to other computers over telephone lines.

29. What is the Internet?
    A. an organized collection of information
    B. a field that holds one type of information
    C. the international web of computer networks
    D. a bunch of computers connected together

30. Which of the following is an input device?
    A. printer
    B. monitor
    C. modem
    D. keyboard

43

Name: _____ Date: _____

Lesson Three: Information Skills (cont.)

Review

1. Read all maps, charts, graphs, and diagrams carefully.

2. It is usually not a good idea to change an answer, as your first guess is usually the correct one.

3. If you <u>must</u> change an answer, be sure to erase your mistake completely.

4. Choose your answers thoughtfully. More than one answer may *seem* correct.

5. Don't look ahead to another question until you complete the one you are working on.

6. Remember, all you can do is your personal best!

Helpful Math Strategies

Test Tips

1. Use all of the time that is provided. This is a test, not a race.
2. Use your time wisely.
3. Do not spend too much time on any one answer.
4. Skip hard questions and do the easy ones first. Then go back and do the hard ones.
5. Read each question carefully.
6. Read the question twice if you have to.

Math Strategies

★   Look at the signs carefully in the problem. Know if you are being asked to add, subtract, multiply, or divide.

★   The right answer may not be given.

★   Check your work by reversing the problem.

★   Do all of your work on scrap paper.

★   Be sure to transfer the correct answer to the answer sheet.

★   Estimate the answer before working the problem.

★   Recognize a reasonable answer, and eliminate those answer choices that are not reasonable.

★   Decide if your answer makes sense.

★   Study the words in word problems carefully to decide what you have to do to find the answer.

Name: _____ Date: _____

UNIT THREE: MATHEMATICS

Lesson One: Concepts

1. The smallest common denominator for a set of fractions is the
   A.   least common multiple.
   B.   least common denominator.
   C.   greatest common multiple.
   D.   greatest common denominator.

2. A line along which you could fold a figure so that both halves match is called a
   A.   line segment.
   B.   line.
   C.   line graph.
   D.   line of symmetry.

3. A polygon with six sides is a
   A.   hexagon.
   B.   pentagon.
   C.   octagon.
   D.   heptagon.

4. In division, the _____ is the answer.
   A.   product
   B.   divisor
   C.   quotient
   D.   dividend

5. The top number of any fraction is called the
   A.   numerator.
   B.   denominator.
   C.   terminator.
   D.   equivalent.

6. The bottom number of any fraction is called the
   A.   numerator.
   B.   denominator.
   C.   terminator.
   D.   equivalent.

Answer the easy questions first.

Name: _____ Date: _____

Lesson One: Concepts (cont.)

7. The _____ are the numbers being added together in an addition problem.
    A. factors
    B. digits
    C. addends
    D. whole numbers

8. If two figures have <u>exactly</u> the same size and shape, they are said to be
    A. diagonal.
    B. equivalent.
    C. intersecting.
    D. congruent.

9. The problem $4 \times (3 + 5) = (4 \times 3) + (4 \times 5)$ demonstrates the _____ property of multiplication.
    A. identity
    B. commutative
    C. distributive
    D. associative

10. Any answer that is not *exact* is a(n)
    A. variable.
    B. odd number.
    C. average.
    D. estimate.

11. In the problem $2 \times (n \times 4) = (2 \times 3) \times 4$,
    A. $n = 2$.
    B. $n = 6$.
    C. $n = 3$.
    D. $n = 24$.

12. In the problem $n \times 5 = 40$,
    A. $n = 6$.
    B. $n = 8$.
    C. $n = 7$.
    D. $n = 9$.

13. Round 3,653 to the nearest hundreds.
    A. 3,700
    B. 3,600
    C. 3,500
    D. 4,000

> Recognize a reasonable answer, and eliminate those answer choices that are <u>not</u> reasonable.

Name: _____   Date: _____

Lesson One: Concepts (cont.)

14. Mr. Halteman owns a small bakery. Last year, his costs were $66,350. He sold $115,849 worth of baked goods. Estimate to the nearest thousand his profit for last year.
    A. $49,000
    B. $49,500
    C. $50,000
    D. $49,499

15. Calculate Mr. Halteman's <u>exact</u> profit.
    A. $49,000
    B. $49,500
    C. $50,000
    D. $49,499

Read each question carefully!

16. Which is an equivalent decimal for 6.2?
    A. 6.02
    B. 6.20
    C. 6.0200
    D. 0.602

17. Which of these has numbers ordered from least to greatest?
    A. 0.26, 0.521, 0.620, 6.252
    B. 0.620, 0.521, 6.252, 0.26
    C. 0.620, 0.26, 6.252, 0.521
    D. 6.252, 0.620, 0.521, 0.26

18. In this series of numbers: 45, 66, 89, 69, 77, 22, 66, which orders the numbers from greatest to least?
    A. 22, 45, 66, 66, 69, 89, 77
    B. 77, 89, 69, 66, 66, 45, 22
    C. 22, 45, 69, 66, 66, 77, 89
    D. 89, 77, 69, 66, 66, 45, 22

19. <u>Range</u> is the difference between greatest and least. In this series of numbers: 45, 66, 89, 69, 77, 22, 66, what is the range?
    A. 67   B. 76   C. 55   D. 88

20. <u>Mean</u> is the average of the numbers. In this series of numbers: 45, 66, 89, 69, 77, 22, 66, what is the mean?
    A. 53   B. 72   C. 62   D. 42

21. <u>Median</u> is the number in the exact middle. In this series of numbers: 45, 66, 89, 69, 77, 22, 66, what is the median?
    A. 69   B. 66   C. 77   D. 45

Name: _____   Date: _____

Lesson One: Concepts (cont.)

22. Four quarts equals how many pints?
    A.   32
    B.   8
    C.   16
    D.   1

23. Three gallons equals how many cups?
    A.   384
    B.   32
    C.   12
    D.   48

Ounces	Cups	Pints	Quarts	Gallons
8	1			
16	2	1		
32	4	2	1	
64	8	4	2	
128	16	8	4	1

24. 250 ounces = _____ cups and _____ ounces?
    A.   31 cups and 2 ounces
    B.   312 cups and 5 ounces
    C.   32 cups and 0 ounces
    D.   25 cups and 0 ounces

25.   7 hours, 37 minutes
    + 6 hours, 32 minutes
    _____

    A.   13 hours, 69 minutes
    B.   14 hours, 9 minutes
    C.   1 hour, 5 minutes
    D.   none of these

Seconds		Minutes		Hours
60	=	1		
3,600	=	60	=	1

26.   2 hours, 29 minutes
    - 1 hour, 30 minutes
    _____

    A.   1 hour, 59 minutes
    B.   59 minutes
    C.   1 hour, 19 minutes
    D.   none of these

27. Which of these is the most appropriate measurement for measuring the length of the Mississippi River?
    A.   mm
    B.   cm
    C.   m
    D.   km

Name: _____   Date: _____

Lesson One: Concepts (cont.)

28. Which of these is the most appropriate measurement for measuring the diameter of a dime?
    A.   mm
    B.   cm
    C.   m
    D.   km

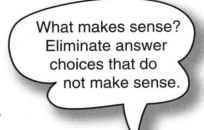

What makes sense? Eliminate answer choices that do not make sense.

29. Which of these is the most appropriate measurement for measuring the amount of water in a swimming pool?
    A.   grams
    B.   liters
    C.   kiloliters
    D.   centiliters

30. Which of these is the most appropriate measurement for measuring the weight of a large dog?
    A.   grams
    B.   milligrams
    C.   kilograms
    D.   liters

Directions: Examine the calculator to the right. Then answer questions 31–35.

---

31. Which of the following indicates the memory key(s)?
    A.   7
    B.   6
    C.   5
    D.   4

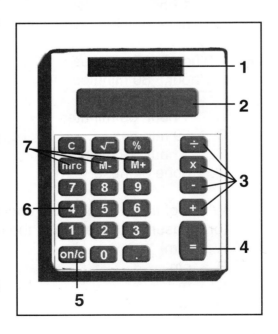

32. If you wanted the answer to the problem 2 x 4, which key would you press to get it?
    A.   1
    B.   2
    C.   3
    D.   4

33. What is the purpose of the *M+* key?
    A.   It is used to multiply the same number several times.
    B.   It saves a number for use later on.
    C.   It is used to find out what is in the calculator's memory.
    D.   It is used to clear the memory from the calculator.

Name: _____ Date: _____

Lesson One: Concepts (cont.)

34. For which of these problems would it be most appropriate to use a calculator?
    A. $5 + 6 + 7$
    B. 267×873
    C. 100×5
    D. $\frac{3}{8} + \frac{2}{3}$

Do not spend too much time on any one problem.

35. The product of 1.5×1.2 is 1.80. How does the calculator show the product?
    A. 18.0
    B. 1.80
    C. 1.8
    D. 18.00

36. Which of these formulas is correct for finding the area of a rectangle?
    A. $A = b \times h$
    B. $A = r^2$
    C. $A = l \times w$
    D. none of these

37. The right angle in the diagram to the right is
    A. ∠BED.
    B. ∠BEC.
    C. ∠AED.
    D. ∠AEC.

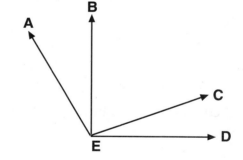

38. The obtuse angle in the diagram to the right is
    A. ∠BED.
    B. ∠BEC.
    C. ∠AED.
    D. ∠CED.

39. The vertex in the diagram to the right is point
    A. B.
    B. C.
    C. D.
    D. E.

40. What is the probability of choosing a cat's-eye marble from this marble jar?
    A. 4 out of 12
    B. 1 out of 14
    C. 8 out of 12
    D. 2 out of 3

A = agate
C = cat's eye
P = purees

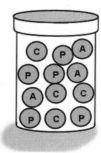

Name: _____   Date: _____

Lesson One: Concepts (cont.)

41. What is the probability of choosing an agate or a cat's eye from the jar?
    A.   6 out of 12
    B.   50%
    C.   7 out of 12
    D.   1 out of 2

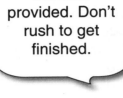

> Use all of the time provided. Don't rush to get finished.

42. What sign is missing in this problem? $\frac{2}{3}$ ◯ $\frac{5}{8}$
    A. $\leq$
    B. $\geq$
    C. $=$
    D. $<$

43. What sign is missing in this problem? $\frac{7}{8}$ ◯ $\frac{2}{5}$
    A. $\leq$
    B. $\geq$
    C. $=$
    D. $<$

44. What sign is missing in this problem? 0.250 ◯ 0.5
    A. $\leq$
    B. $\geq$
    C. $=$
    D. $>$

45. Using the chart to the right, what percentage of students chose pizza?
    A.   20%
    B.   40%
    C.   10%
    D.   6%

FAVORITE LUNCH CHOICES	
Hamburgers	234
Hot dogs	358
Pizza	586
Sandwiches	172
Salad	87
	1,437

46. What percentage of students chose salad?
    A.   20%
    B.   40%
    C.   10%
    D.   6%

Name: _____   Date: _____

Lesson One: Concepts (cont.)

Directions: Examine the international clocks in this diagram, and then answer the questions.

7 A.M. in Lima, Peru	Noon in London, England	1 P.M. in Oslo, Norway	2 P.M. in Cairo, Egypt	3 P.M. in Moscow, Russia	7 P.M. in Jakarta, Indonesia	8 P.M. in Hong Kong, China

47. Which is the correct order from <u>earliest</u> to <u>latest</u>?
    A.   London, Moscow, Jakarta, Oslo
    B.   Lima, London, Cairo, Hong Kong
    C.   Hong Kong, Jakarta, Cairo, New York
    D.   Lima, London, Hong Kong, Cairo

48. What is the time difference between Lima and Hong Kong?
    A.   1 hour
    B.   12 hours
    C.   13 hours
    D.   3 hours

Directions: The bar graph on the following page shows the most popular websites among the students in one school. Use this data to answer questions 49–50.

49. How many more students looked up Earth Day than Egypt?
    A.   114
    B.   104
    C.   158
    D.   100

50. How many students looked up something other than Earth Day?
    A.   263
    B.   255
    C.   96
    D.   132

Name: _____   Date: _____

Lesson One: Concepts (cont.)

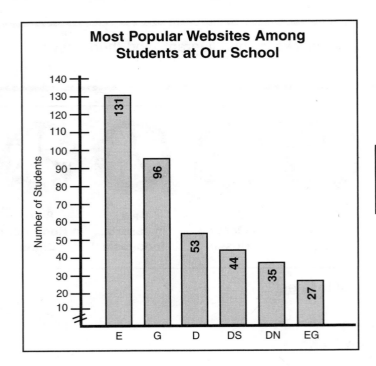

Most Popular Websites Among Students at Our School

(Number of Students)

E = 131
G = 96
D = 53
DS = 44
DN = 35
EG = 27

E   G   D   DS   DN   EG

E = Earth Day   DS = Disney
G = Games   DN = Dinosaurs
D = Dogs   EG = Egypt

Review

1. Answer the easy questions first!

2. Recognize a reasonable answer, and eliminate those answer choices that are <u>not</u> reasonable.

3. Read each question very carefully.

4. Do not spend too much time on any one problem.

5. What makes sense? Eliminate answer choices that do not make sense.

6. Use all of the time that is provided. Don't rush to get finished.

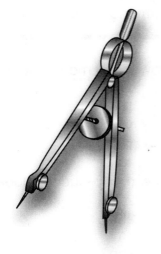

Name: _____ Date: _____

UNIT THREE: MATHEMATICS

Lesson Two: Computation

1. What is the numeral for four thousand, three hundred twenty-three?
   A. 4322
   B. 4323
   C. 43323
   D. 40323

2. What is the numeral for one hundred fifty-seven thousand, sixty one?
   A. 100570061
   B. 150700061
   C. 157610
   D. 157061

3. 2435 in expanded notation is
   A. 24000 + 30 + 5
   B. 2000 + 43 + 5
   C. 2000 + 400 + 30 + 5
   D. 2 x 100 + 4 x 10 + 3 x 5

4. What number is 600000 + 80000 + 1000 + 700 + 90 + 4?
   A. 681794
   B. 148000794
   C. 690497
   D. 881794

5. Which of these numbers is <u>not</u> a prime number?
   A. 2
   B. 3
   C. 4
   D. 5

6. Which of these numbers <u>is</u> a prime number?
   A. 25
   B. 33
   C. 48
   D. 59

Use your time wisely, but don't rush.

Name: _____ Date: _____

Lesson Two: Computation (cont.)

7. The planet Mercury is 3.6×10^7 miles from the sun. Which of these numbers means the same as 10^7?
   A. $10 + 10 + 10 + 10 + 10 + 10 + 10$
   B. $10 \times 10 \times 10 \times 10 \times 10 \times 10 \times 10$
   C. 100×7
   D. $1{,}000 \times 7$

8. What is the value of the underlined digit?   351.38<u>6</u>
   A. 6 ones
   B. 6 tenths
   C. 6 hundredths
   D. 6 thousandths

9. What is the value of the underlined digit?   2.9<u>3</u>6
   A. 3 ones
   B. 3 tenths
   C. 3 hundredths
   D. 3 thousandths

10. Which is the word name for this decimal?   39.01
    A. Thirty-nine and one hundredth
    B. Three hundred and nine thousandths
    C. Thirty-nine and one tenth
    D. Thirty-nine and one thousandth

11. Which is the decimal for fourteen and six thousandths?
    A. 1.4006
    B. 140.06
    C. 14.006
    D. 14.60

12. The sum of 32.49 + 14.75 =
    A. 39.74
    B. 54.49
    C. 47.24
    D. none of these

13. $16.99 + $142.25 + $189 + $34.59 =
    A. $400.00
    B. $380.83
    C. $382.83
    D. none of these

> Recognize a reasonable answer, and eliminate those that are not reasonable.

Name: _____   Date: _____

Lesson Two: Computation (cont.)

14. 9.75 kg + 6.8 kg + 10.035 kg =
   A.   10.978
   B.   26.585
   C.   15.595
   D.   none of these

15.   523.06
     + 399.19

   A.   822.25
   B.   921.35
   C.   920.50
   D.   none of these

16.   5.214 km
     - 0.062 km

   A.   51.52
   B.   5.152
   C.   515.2
   D.   none of these

17. 796.1 - 7.86 =

   A.   788.24
   B.   803.96
   C.   717.50
   D.   none of these

18. 3,869.101 - 3,573.92 =

   A.   29.5181
   B.   2951.81
   C.   295.181
   D.   none of these

19.   261,431
     - 176,469

   A.   83,962
   B.   84,862
   C.   84,972
   D.   none of these

20.   176.112
       812.354
     +   2.872

   A.   891.338
   B.   991.338
   C.   990.338
   D.   none of these

21. 12 is a common multiple of all but
   A.   6
   B.   5
   C.   4
   D.   3

22. Find the LCM of (3, 7).
   A.   15
   B.   18
   C.   21
   D.   24

23. Find the LCM of (2, 4, 5).
   A.   10
   B.   8
   C.   4
   D.   none of these

24. 65 x 18 =
   A.   83
   B.   1,170
   C.   1,270
   D.   none of these

25. 652 x 13 =
   A.   9,476
   B.   8,467
   C.   8,476
   D.   none of these

Estimate your answer before working the problem.

Name: _____ Date: _____

Lesson Two: Computation (cont.)

26. 1,034 x 697 =

    A.   721,798
    B.   720,699
    C.   720,698
    D.   none of these

27. 325 x 210 =

    A.   69,250
    B.   68,340
    C.   68,250
    D.   none of these

28. 5,278 x 2,885 =

    A.   15,227,030
    B.   15,327,030
    C.   15722,030
    D.   none of these

29. 3,256 ÷ 8 =

    A.   409
    B.   507
    C.   407
    D.   none of these

30. $5 \overline{)35,005}$

    A.   6,001
    B.   7,001
    C.   7,000
    D.   none

31. $3 \overline{)9,054}$

    A.   3,018
    B.   318
    C.   3,180
    D.   none of these

32. 702 ÷ 9 =

    A.   79
    B.   78
    C.   68
    D.   none of these

33. 12,044 ÷ 6 =

    A.   2,007
    B.   2,007 R3
    C.   2,007 R2
    D.   none of these

34. $\frac{729}{4}$

    A.   182
    B.   18 R21
    C.   1,821
    D.   none of these

35. 47,888 ÷ 29 =

    A.   1,561 R9
    B.   1,615 R2
    C.   1,651 R9
    D.   none of these

36. Which is an equivalent fraction for $\frac{9}{12}$?

    A. $\frac{1}{2}$
    B. $\frac{2}{3}$
    C. $\frac{3}{4}$
    D.   none of these

37. Which is an equivalent fraction for $\frac{7}{8}$?

    A. $\frac{1}{8}$
    B. $\frac{4}{6}$
    C. $\frac{14}{16}$
    D.   none of these

Name: _____ Date: _____

Lesson Two: Computation (cont.)

38. $\frac{2}{8} = \frac{4}{n}$
   A. $n = 16$
   B. $n = 8$
   C. $n = 2$
   D. none of these

39. Which is the simplest form of $\frac{24}{30}$?
   A. $\frac{8}{10}$
   B. $\frac{4}{5}$
   C. $\frac{2}{30}$
   D. none of these

40. Which is the simplest form of $\frac{12}{16}$?

   A. $\frac{2}{4}$
   B. $\frac{3}{4}$
   C. $\frac{9}{12}$
   D. none of these

41. Which is <u>not</u> equivalent to $\frac{1}{4}$?
   A. $\frac{6}{24}$
   B. $\frac{3}{12}$
   C. $\frac{4}{12}$
   D. none of these

42. $4 = \frac{n}{8}$
   A. $n = 32$
   B. $n = 8$
   C. $n = 5$
   D. none of these

43. $1\frac{3}{12} - \frac{n}{12} = \frac{3}{12}$
   A. $n = 12$
   B. $n = 15$
   C. $n = 3$
   D. none of these

44. Change $\frac{23}{6}$ to a mixed number in simplest form.
   A. $1\frac{11}{6}$
   B. $3\frac{5}{6}$
   C. $2\frac{11}{6}$
   D. none of these

45. $\frac{2}{5} + \frac{9}{10} =$
   A. $\frac{11}{10}$
   B. $1\frac{3}{10}$
   C. $\frac{11}{15}$
   D. none of these

46. $\frac{2}{8} + \frac{2}{6} =$
   A. $\frac{14}{24}$
   B. $\frac{4}{14}$
   C. $\frac{16}{24}$
   D. none of these

47. $\frac{5}{6} - \frac{2}{10} =$
   A. $\frac{3}{16}$
   B. $\frac{31}{30}$
   C. $\frac{19}{30}$
   D. none of these

48. $\frac{3}{5} - \frac{1}{3} =$
   A. $\frac{4}{15}$
   B. $\frac{2}{15}$
   C. $\frac{2}{2}$
   D. none of these

49. $3\frac{1}{4} + 2\frac{1}{8} =$
   A. $7\frac{1}{8}$
   B. $5\frac{7}{8}$
   C. $5\frac{3}{8}$
   D. none of these

Look at the signs carefully. Know what operation you are being asked to perform.

Name: _____ Date: _____

Lesson Two: Computation (cont.)

50. $1\frac{2}{5} + 6\frac{3}{6} =$
  A. $7\frac{27}{30}$
  B. $7\frac{5}{6}$
  C. $5\frac{27}{30}$
  D.   none of these

51. $4\frac{3}{4} + 1\frac{2}{5} + 3\frac{1}{10} =$
  A. $8\frac{5}{20}$
  B. $9\frac{1}{4}$
  C. $8\frac{1}{4}$
  D.   none of these

52. $9\frac{2}{3} - 3\frac{1}{5} =$
  A. $6\frac{13}{15}$
  B. $7\frac{13}{15}$
  C. $5\frac{7}{15}$
  D.   none of these

53. $6\frac{4}{5} - 1\frac{2}{7} =$
  A. $7\frac{31}{35}$
  B. $5\frac{18}{35}$
  C. $5\frac{31}{35}$
  D.   none of these

54. $\frac{7}{8} \times \frac{3}{4} =$
  A. $\frac{21}{32}$
  B. $\frac{11}{12}$
  C. $\frac{5}{6}$
  D.   none of these

55. $6\frac{2}{3} \times 5\frac{1}{4} =$
  A. $30\frac{2}{3}$
  B. 32
  C. 35
  D.   none of these

56. $\frac{4}{5} \div \frac{3}{8} =$
  A. $2\frac{2}{15}$
  B. $\frac{30}{15}$
  C. $\frac{12}{40}$
  D.   none of these

57. $2\frac{1}{2} \div 1\frac{1}{4} =$
  A. 3
  B. $\frac{2}{5}$
  C. $\frac{5}{10}$
  D.   none of these

58. What number equals the fraction $\frac{4}{5}$?
  A.   0.8
  B.   8
  C.   0.85
  D.   none of these

59. What is 30% of 90?
  A.   27
  B.   30
  C.   40
  D.   none of these

60. 18 is 20% of what number?
  A.   90
  B.   80
  C.   70
  D.   none of these

Be sure to check your work. The right answer may not be given.

Name: _____ Date: _____

Lesson Two: Computation (cont.)

Review

1. Use your time wisely.

2. Recognize a reasonable answer and eliminate those answer choices that are <u>not</u> reasonable.

3. Estimate your answer before working the problem.

4. Look at the signs carefully. Know what operation you are expected to perform.

5. Be sure to check your work. The right answer may not be given.

Name: _____   Date: _____

UNIT THREE: MATHEMATICS

Lesson Three: Problem Solving and Reasoning

1. Royce and Rudi had lunch together in a restaurant. Royce's entree cost $12.95, and Rudi's cost $15.95. Both had apple pie for dessert, which cost an additional $2.90 each. How much was the total bill?

     A. $34.70
     B. $35.00
     C. $37.30
     D.   none of these

2. Given their bill above, Royce and Rudi wanted to leave a 20% tip for their waiter. About how much should they leave?

     A. $2.00
     B. $4.00
     C. $7.00
     D.   none of these

3. One Cardinals pitcher can throw a ball 111.45 miles per hour. Another pitcher throws a 97.6 mph pitch. What is the difference in speed between the two pitchers?

     A.   138.5 mph
     B.   13.85 mph
     C.   1.385 mph
     D.   none of these

4. May was a very rainy month in Peabody Township. The weekly rainfall during May was 1.8 inches, 4.6 inches, 6.9 inches, and 4.5 inches. What was the total rainfall in May?

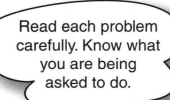

Read each problem carefully. Know what you are being asked to do.

     A.   17.8 inches
     B.   1.78 inches
     C.   178 inches
     D.   none of these

5. About how much was the <u>average</u> weekly rainfall in May?

     A.   450 inches
     B.   44.5 inches
     C.   4.5 inches
     D.   none of these

Name: _____ Date: _____

Lesson Three: Problem Solving and Reasoning (cont.)

6. Elysia wants to buy a new CD that costs $19.99. She only has $17.83. How much more does she need?

   A. $21.60
   B. $2.16
   C.   21¢
   D.   none of these

7. Kelly scored 9.6 on technical merit and 9.8 on artistic merit in her ice-skating competition. Her scores were averaged for her overall score. She was outscored by Mandy whose overall score was 0.25 better than Kelly's. What was Mandy's overall score?

   A.   9.80
   B.   9.95
   C.   9.75
   D.   none of these

8. Ramón worked at McDonald's for $7.25 per hour. Last week, he worked 35 hours. How much did he earn?

   A. $253.75
   B. $25.37
   C. $263.75
   D.   none of these

9. The government took 10% of Ramón's earnings for taxes. How much did he get to keep?

   A. $253.75
   B. $208.38
   C. $228.38
   D.   none of these

10. Karl earned a 94% on his 50-problem math test. How many problems did he miss?

   A.   4
   B.   3
   C.   2
   D.   none of these

Read each problem twice if you have to.

      63

Name: _____ Date: _____

Lesson Three: Problem Solving and Reasoning (cont.)

11. Seven more than what number equals twenty-one?

    A.   28
    B.   147
    C.   14
    D.   none of these

12. Seven less than what number equals twenty-one?

    A.   28
    B.   147
    C.   14
    D.   none of these

Decide if your answers make sense.

13. Seven times what number equals twenty-one?

    A.   147
    B.   3
    C.   14
    D.   none of these

14. What number divided by seven equals twenty-one?

    A.   147
    B.   3
    C.   14
    D.   none of these

15. If a half-pound of Gummy Bears costs $1.80, what would a whole pound of Gummy Bears cost?

    A.   36¢
    B. $3.60
    C. $36.00
    D.   none of these

16. New soccer uniforms for the team cost $800. The team has earned $600 so far. What fraction of the cost have they earned so far?

    A. $\frac{1}{4}$
    B. $\frac{1}{2}$
    C. $\frac{3}{4}$
    D.   none of these

Lesson Three: Problem Solving and Reasoning (cont.)

17. The fifth grade donated 30% of the $150 they earned from a recent bake sale to a local charity. How much money did they donate?

    A. $50
    B. $75
    C. $100
    D.   none of these

18. 70% of the 60 members of the football team voted Nathan Most Valuable Player. How many players voted for Nathan?

    A.   38
    B.   60
    C.   42
    D.   none of these

19. The mall opens at 10:00 A.M. and closes at 8:00 P.M. For how many hours each day is the mall open?

    A.   10 hours
    B.   12 hours
    C.   8 hours
    D.   none of these

20. Kate started watching a movie at 7:15 P.M. It was $2\frac{1}{2}$ hours long. What time did she finish watching the movie?

    A.   9:15 P.M.
    B.   9:45 P.M.
    C.   9:30 P.M.
    D.   none of these

21. Twenty-four more than what number is forty-three?

    A.   24
    B.   19
    C.   67
    D.   none of these

Skip hard questions and answer the easy ones first.

Lesson Three: Problem Solving and Reasoning (cont.)

22. Nine more than what number equals 54?

    A.   45
    B.   6
    C.   63
    D.   none of these

23. Nine less than what number equals 54?

    A.   45
    B.   6
    C.   63
    D.   none of these

24. Nine times what number equals 54?

    A.   45
    B.   6
    C.   63
    D.   none of these

25. What number divided by 9 equals 54?

    A.   54
    B.   81
    C.   486
    D.   none of these

26. Two thirds of what number equals 54?

    A.   54
    B.   81
    C.   486
    D.   none of these

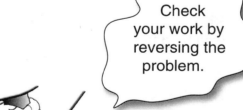

Check your work by reversing the problem.

27. Which number sentence means "The sum of two times a number (*n*) and two equals eighteen"?

    A. $2n - 2 = 18$
    B. $2n + 2 = 18$
    C. $2n \times 2 = 18$
    D.   none of these

Name: _____ Date: _____

Lesson Three: Problem Solving and Reasoning (cont.)

28. Which number sentence means, "The product of a number (*n*) and three equals twenty-one"?
    A.　$n \times 3 = 21$
    B.　$n \div 3 = 21$
    C.　$n + 3 = 21$
    D.　none of these

29. What is the volume of a box with a length of 2.8, a width of 3.2, and a height of 6.5?
    A.　58.25 cubic units
    B.　58.24 cubic units
    C.　5.84 cubic units
    D.　none of these

Do all calculations on scratch paper, but transfer your answer carefully to the answer sheet.

30. Tasha runs 5 miles per day in all kinds of weather, even in the winter months. How many miles does Tasha run in November?
    A.　100 miles
    B.　150 miles
    C.　1,500 miles
    D.　none of these

31. Stephen saved 2,680 pennies. If there are 50 pennies per roll, how many penny wrappers does Stephen need?
    A.　53
    B.　54
    C.　50
    D.　none of these

32. There are 12 months in a year. What is the probability that a month chosen at random will begin with the letter M?
    A.　$\frac{3}{12}$　　　　C.　$\frac{9}{12}$
    B.　$\frac{2}{12}$　　　　D.　none of these

33. Carmen made peanut butter cookies. She gave Marcie half of them. Marcie shared the cookies equally with her two brothers. How many cookies did Carmen make if Marcie and her two brothers each got 12 cookies?
    A.　36　　　　C.　72
    B.　24　　　　D.　none of these

Name: _____ Date: _____

Lesson Three: Problem Solving and Reasoning (cont.)

34. Jack wanted to enter the longest running race in his area. One race was 5 kilometers (km). Another was 700 meters (m), and a third was 6,500 meters. Which race should he enter?

    A. 5 km
    B. 700 m
    C. 6,500 m
    D. none of these

35. Mrs. Steiner wants to frame her son's diploma. It measures 8″ x 11″. How many inches of wood does she need?

    A. 88
    B. 32
    C. 48
    D. none of these

Review

1. Read each problem carefully. Know what you are being asked to do.

2. Read each problem twice if you have to.

3. Decide if your answer makes sense.

4. Skip the hard questions and answer the easy ones first.

5. Do all calculations on scratch paper, but transfer your answer carefully to the answer sheet.

Helpful Science Strategies

Test Tips

1. Work as quickly as you can.
2. Skip the hard questions and answer the easy ones first; go back to the hard questions when you finish.
3. Answer all questions; when all else fails, guess!
4. Think twice before changing an answer; your first guess is usually the correct one.
5. If you change an answer, be sure to erase your pencil marks completely.
6. Often information in a later question can be used to answer an earlier question.
7. Pay attention to key words like *not, but, except, always, never,* and *only*.

Science Strategies

★ Science test questions usually cover information about life science, physical science, earth science, and health science.

★ Pay attention to important words in each question that might make the answer choices true or untrue.

★ Pay close attention to how the questions are worded. All answers may be *true,* but only <u>one</u> answers the question.

★ Keep in mind the steps of the scientific process.

★ Use logical reasoning to answer the questions. Does your answer make sense?

★ Use the process of elimination to find answers. Cross out those that you *know* are wrong.

★ Examine charts, pictures, diagrams, and figures carefully.

Name: _____ Date: _____

UNIT FOUR: SCIENCE

Lesson One: Process and Inquiry

1. What does the word <u>science</u> mean?
   A. the art of studying everything around us
   B. the art of studying living things
   C. the systematic study of animals
   D. a method of observation

A. 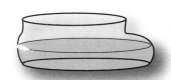   B.    C. 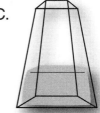   D.

Figure 1

2. Which jar in Figure 1 will lose water faster to evaporation?
   A. A   C. C
   B. B   D. D

3. Which thermometer in Figure 2 records the coldest temperature?
   A. A   C. C
   B. B   D. D

4. What is the hottest temperature shown?
   A. 45°   C. 20°
   B. 0°   D. -10°

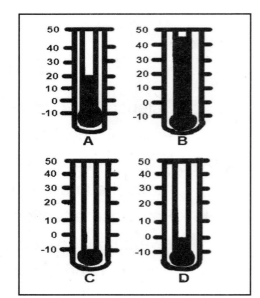

Figure 2

Science test questions usually cover information about life science, physical science, earth science, and health science.

Name: _____ Date: _____

Lesson One: Process and Inquiry (cont.)

5. What is inside a thermometer?
    A.   a liquid that goes up and down
    B.   a liquid very sensitive to changes in temperature
    C.   a liquid that changes color with temperature changes
    D.   two liquids, one reacts to hot, the other to cold

6. Are our bodies colder or warmer than the air around us?
    A.   colder
    B.   warmer
    C.   the same
    D.   neither

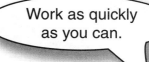

Work as quickly as you can.

7. Why does a wet hand feel colder than a dry hand?
    A.   The dry hand is warmer than the wet hand.
    B.   The wet hand is warmer than the air around it.
    C.   The dry hand is dryer than the wet hand.
    D.   The wet hand is colder than the air around it.

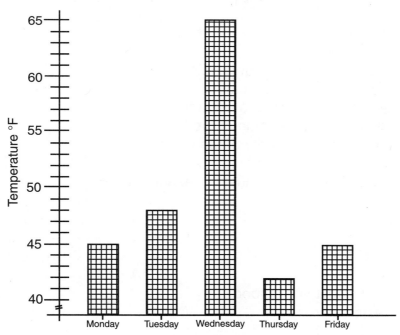

Figure 3

8. Examine the data collected by one group of students in Figure 3. What is the most likely explanation for the sudden rise in temperature on Wednesday?
    A.   The thermometer was broken on Wednesday.
    B.   They used a different thermometer.
    C.   They measured at a later time of the day.
    D.   They measured inside the classroom.

Name: _____ Date: _____

Lesson One: Process and Inquiry (cont.)

Directions: Examine the diagram (Figure 4) and the chart carefully.

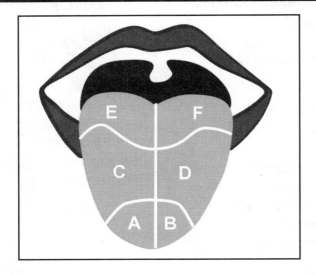

chips B	lemon C	p. butter B
banana A	apple E	vinegar D
candy A	radish E	strawberry A
pretzel B	cabbage E	pineapple A

Figure 4

9. What conclusion could you draw from this data?
    A. Sweet and salty taste buds are located at the front of the tongue.
    B. Sour and bitter taste buds are located at the front of the tongue.
    C. Sweet taste buds are in the middle of the tongue.
    D. Bitter taste buds are in the middle of the tongue.

10. To really taste the flavor of food, you must be able to
    A. feel it.
    B. see it.
    C. smell it.
    D. touch it.

Use the process of elimination to find answers. Eliminate those you know are wrong.

11. Does color affect the *actual* taste of food?
    A. Yes, you can taste color.
    B. Yes, the color affects what you think about the food.
    C. No, color has no taste.
    D. No, color only changes the smell, not the taste.

Name: _____   Date: _____

Lesson One: Process and Inquiry (cont.)

OBSERVATION: On a two-week camping trip, Dad refused to shower or take a bath. Mom showered every other day. At the end of the camping trip, Mom was one giant mosquito bite; she had too many bites to count. Dad, however, was virtually bite-free.

---

12. Read Bob's observation above. Which of the choices below is a workable hypothesis that could be used in an experiment to test some aspect of the observation?
    A.   The camping trip was too long.
    B.   Dad really smelled after two weeks.
    C.   Mosquitoes are drawn to a clean smell.
    D.   Even the mosquitoes wouldn't go near Dad.

Directions: These animals have special body parts that help them survive. For questions 13–17, choose the animal that matches the description.

| squirrel | bat | raccoon | woodpecker | badger |

Figure 5

13. Which animal uses its sharp teeth to crack nuts?
    A.   squirrel
    B.   bat
    C.   badger
    D.   raccoon

Answer all questions. If all else fails, guess!

14. Which animal uses echoes to find and eat insects in the air?
    A.   squirrel
    B.   bat
    C.   badger
    D.   woodpecker

Name: _____   Date: _____

Lesson One: Process and Inquiry (cont.)

15. Which animal uses its handlike paws to catch and eat fish and frogs?
    A. woodpecker
    B. bat
    C. badger
    D. raccoon

16. Which animal uses its pointed beak to dig under tree bark for insects?
    A. squirrel
    B. bat
    C. woodpecker
    D. raccoon

Use logical reasoning to answer the questions. Does your answer choice make sense?

17. Which animal uses its long, curved claws to dig tunnels to look for rodents?
    A. squirrel
    B. bat
    C. badger
    D. raccoon

Forest   Desert   Tundra   Savanna

Figure 6

18. What is the habitat of a snowy owl?
    A. forest
    B. desert
    C. tundra
    D. savanna

19. What is the habitat of a garter snake?
    A. forest
    B. desert
    C. tundra
    D. savanna

20. What is the habitat of a spotted leopard?
    A. forest
    B. desert
    C. tundra
    D. savanna

Name: _____ Date: _____

Lesson One: Process and Inquiry (cont.)

WEIGHT TABLE (pounds)										
Ages	0–1	1–3	3–6	6–9	9–12	12–15	15–18	18–35	35–55	55–75
Male	18	29	40	53	72	98	134	154	154	154
Female	18	29	40	53	72	103	117	128	128	128

Figure 7

21. What conclusion can be drawn from the above weight table?
    A. Babies don't weigh very much.
    B. Boys weigh much more than girls.
    C. Girls and boys weigh about the same.
    D. Between ages 12–15, girls weigh more than boys.

HEIGHT TABLE (inches)									
Ages	1–3	3–6	6–9	9–12	12–15	15–18	18–35	35–55	55–75
Male	34	42	49	55	61	68	69	69	69
Female	34	42	49	55	62	64	64	64	64

Figure 8

22. What conclusion can be drawn from the above height table?
    A. Boys are much taller than girls in elementary school.
    B. Girls are taller than boys in the early teen years.
    C. All men are taller than all women.
    D. The older a man gets, the taller he gets.

23. Which of these is a hypothesis?
    A. Why are bees always around flowers?
    B. Bees sting.
    C. How does nectar turn into honey?
    D. Bees are more attracted to sweet-smelling flowers.

75

Name: _____ Date: _____

Lesson One: Process and Inquiry (cont.)

> HYPOTHESIS: There are twice as many brown M&Ms™ in each bag as any other color.

24. How would you design an experiment to test this hypothesis?
    A. Have each group open a bag and count the number of brown M&Ms™ in the bag.
    B. Have each group count the number of each of the other colors in the bag.
    C. Have each group count the number of each color and calculate the percentage of each.
    D. Have each group eat the M&Ms™.

25. A group of students is checking how many senses they use as they pop popcorn and eat it. What important science skill are they using?
    A. experimenting
    B. measuring
    C. predicting
    D. observing

Review

1. Science test questions usually cover information about life science, physical science, earth science, and health science.

2. Work as quickly as you can.

3. Skip the hard questions, and answer the easy ones first.

4. Use the process of elimination to find answers. Eliminate those you know are wrong.

5. Answer all questions. If all else fails, guess!

6. Use logical reasoning to answer the questions. Does your answer choice make sense?

Name: _____ Date: _____

UNIT FOUR: SCIENCE

Lesson Two: Concepts

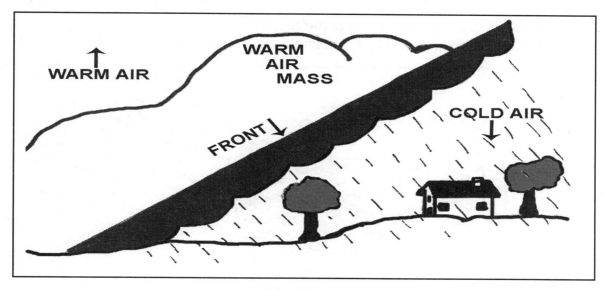

Figure 1

1. Examine Figure 1. What happens when warm and cold air meet?
   A. Cool air sinks and contracts.
   B. The wind picks up speed and changes direction.
   C. Turbulence occurs.
   D. Air moves parallel to the ground.

2. Where does rain come from?
   A. Most of it comes from the sea.
   B. Most of it comes from the clouds.
   C. Most of it comes from the air.
   D. Most of it comes from the sky.

> Pay attention to important words in each question that might make the answer choices true or untrue.

3. What causes changes in weather?
   A. temperature of the air
   B. wind
   C. air pressure
   D. all of the above

4. The amount of moisture in the air is known as
   A. air pressure.
   B. humidity.
   C. barometer.
   D. rain.

Name: _____   Date: _____

Lesson Two: Concepts (cont.)

5. How are hurricanes different from tornadoes?
    A. Hurricanes form over water, tornadoes over land.
    B. Hurricanes are more deadly.
    C. Tornadoes are hurricanes that come ashore.
    D. Tornadoes are warm winds; hurricanes are cold winds.

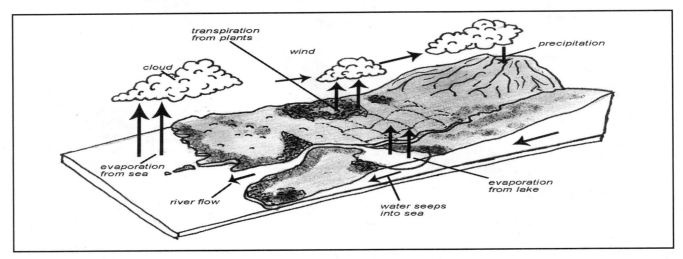

Figure 2

6. Examine Figure 2. Where does the water cycle begin?
    A. with the heat from the sun
    B. when precipitation occurs
    C. when moist warm air rises from the hot water
    D. There is no beginning or end, the cycle just continues over and over.

7. What happens to the water in the ocean?
    A. Nothing, it stays just the same.
    B. The heat from the sun and air evaporates some of it.
    C. When the weather gets cooler, the ocean turns to ice.
    D. When the ocean holds too much water, the water turns into clouds.

8. Where does the water in the ocean come from?
    A. underground fissures
    B. Rain falls into streams that flow into rivers that empty into oceans.
    C. from the snow on top of the mountains
    D. from the water vapor collected in clouds

9. Animals with backbones are called
    A. invertebrates.
    B. vertebrates.
    C. crustaceans.
    D. amphibians.

Keep in mind the scientific process.

Name: _____ Date: _____

Lesson Two: Concepts (cont.)

10. The largest group of invertebrates are
    A.   mollusks.
    B.   arthropods.
    C.   crustaceans.
    D.   amphibians.

Pay attention to key words like *not, but, except, always, never,* and *only.*

11. _____ eat and live in or on plants and animals.
    A.   Parasites
    B.   Invertebrates
    C.   Vertebrates
    D.   Arthropods

12. Why must amphibians spend part of their lives in or near water?
    A.   They breathe through lungs.
    B.   They have webbed feet.
    C.   The eggs they lay would dry out quickly on land.
    D.   They don't have scales.

13. A turtle habitat should include sand, rock, water, and
    A.   shade.
    B.   food.
    C.   toys.
    D.   a cage.

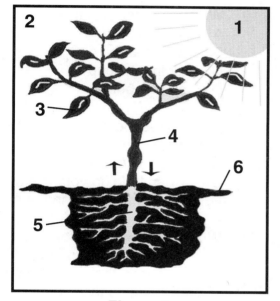

Figure 3

14. Examine Figure 3. What part of the plant transports food, water, and minerals?
    A. 3   B. 4   C. 5   D. 6

15. What part of the plant provides it with food?
    A. 3   B. 4   C. 5   D. 6

16. The sun provides _____ for plants to make their own food.
    A.   warmth
    B.   carbon dioxide
    C.   energy
    D.   chlorophyll

Often, information in a later question can be used to answer an earlier question.

17. *Stem* is to *plant* as _____ is/are to *human.*
    A.   blood vessels
    B.   phlegm
    C.   saliva
    D.   arms

Name: _____ Date: _____

Lesson Two: Concepts (cont.)

18. Examine the heart diagram (Figure 4). In what order does the blood flow through the heart?
    A. ABCD
    B. ACBD
    C. CABD
    D. DBAC

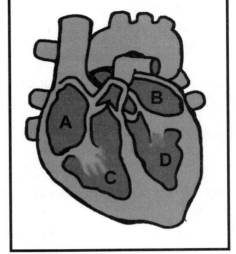

Figure 4

19. Which of these has more carbon dioxide?
    A. air breathed in
    B. air breathed out
    C. air in a hiccup
    D. air in a burp

20. When does the diaphragm contract?
    A. when inhaling
    B. when exhaling
    C. when holding your breath
    D. when you get hit in the stomach

21. Why is smoking bad for your health?
    A. It deposits tar and other substances into the lungs.
    B. It causes the air sacs in the lungs to break apart.
    C. It causes cancer.
    D. All of the above.

22. Examine Figure 5. Number 4 is the earth's
    A. outer core.
    B. mantle.
    C. inner core.
    D. crust.

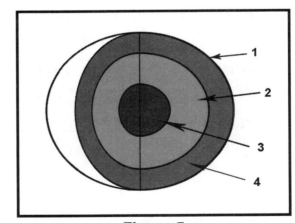

Figure 5

23. Number 3 is the earth's
    A. outer core.
    B. mantle.
    C. inner core.
    D. crust.

24. In which layer are you most likely to find fossils?
    A. outer core
    B. mantle
    C. inner core
    D. crust

Name: _____ Date: _____

Lesson Two: Concepts (cont.)

25. Fossils form when
    A.   the bodies of dead organisms are buried in sediment.
    B.   magma reaches the surface of the earth and cools.
    C.   the crust either bends, cracks, or breaks.
    D.   the remains of plants accumulate in swamps.

26. From the earth's rock, we can learn all but which one?
    A.   about changes in the earth's surface
    B.   about changes in the earth's climate
    C.   about organisms living long ago
    D.   about nonanimal life on Earth

> Pay attention to *how* the questions are worded. All answers might be *true*, but only one answers the question.

27. Which of these does not belong to the Precambrian Era?
    A.   volcanoes
    B.   jellyfish
    C.   dinosaurs
    D.   crabs

28. According to the information in Figure 6, which of these vertebrates has been on Earth the longest?
    A.   amphibians
    B.   reptiles
    C.   fish
    D.   mammals

29. According to the information in Figure 6, which of these vertebrates has been on Earth the shortest amount of time?
    A.   mammals
    B.   birds
    C.   reptiles
    D.   fish

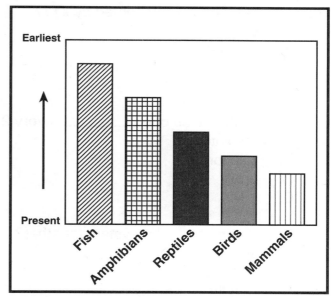

Figure 6

30. From where does almost all of the energy used on Earth originally come?
    A.   nuclear power plants
    B.   fossil fuels
    C.   the sun
    D.   water

Name: _____ Date: _____

Lesson Two: Concepts (cont.)

31. Which of these is not a way to save energy at home?
    A.   turn down the heat
    B.   turn off the lights when not in use
    C.   leave the computer on when not in use
    D.   conserve hot water

32. Examine Figure 7. What type of energy is illustrated?
    A.   kinetic energy
    B.   potential energy
    C.   nuclear energy
    D.   solar energy

Figure 7

33. Examine Figure 8. What season is represented by #4?
    A.   spring
    B.   summer
    C.   fall
    D.   winter

34. What season is represented by #1?
    A.   spring
    B.   summer
    C.   fall
    D.   winter

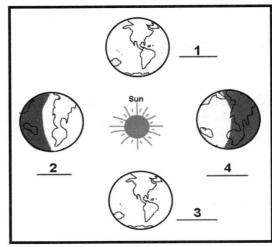

Figure 8

35. The earth makes one _____ every 24 hours.
    A.   revolution
    B.   rotation
    C.   orbit
    D.   turn

36. What keeps our solar system together?
    A.   space
    B.   atmosphere
    C.   gravity
    D.   the pull of the sun

Examine all charts, pictures, diagrams, and figures carefully.

37. _____, sometimes called "dirty snowballs," are huge chunks of ice.
    A.   Comets
    B.   Asteroids
    C.   Satellites
    D.   Constellations

Name: _____ Date: _____

Lesson Two: Concepts (cont.)

38. The center of the solar system is
    A.   Earth.
    B.   the sun.
    C.   a black hole.
    D.   the universe.

39. Which of these space objects is the largest?
    A.   planet
    B.   asteroid
    C.   star
    D.   meteor

40. Which planet in our solar system is best-known for having rings?
    A.   Pluto
    B.   Neptune
    C.   Uranus
    D.   Saturn

If you change an answer, be sure to erase your pencil marks completely.

Review

1. Pay attention to important words in each question that might make the answer choices true or untrue.

2. Keep in mind the steps of the scientific process.

3. Pay attention to key words like *not, but, except, always, never,* and *only*.

4. Often, information in a later question can be used to answer an earlier question.

5. Pay attention to how the questions are worded. All answers may be *true*, but only *one* answers the question.

6. Examine all charts, pictures, diagrams, and figures carefully.

7. If you change an answer, be sure to erase your pencil marks completely.

Helpful Social Studies Strategies

Test Tips

1. Control your test anxiety. Take deep, deep breaths to calm your nervous energy.

2. Don't panic; you are not supposed to know *everything* on the test.

3. Stay calm and focused. Don't let your mind wander.

4. Read and consider all answer choices; there may be a better answer farther down the list, so don't be too anxious.

Social Studies Strategies

★   Social studies is about people, places, and events and when and how they happened.

★   Social studies tests usually include questions about history, geography, culture, government, and economics.

★   Social studies tests also examine your map, graph, and diagram skills.

★   Read maps, graphs, tables, and data charts carefully.

★   When you read a map, be sure to read the title first. Understand the kind of information the map is giving you.

★   Use your time wisely. Answer the ones you know first, and then go back and do the hard ones.

Name: _____ Date: _____

UNIT FIVE: SOCIAL STUDIES

Lesson One: History and Culture

1. Which of these famous songs did Francis Scott Key write?
   A. "America the Beautiful"
   B. "The Star-Spangled Banner"
   C. "You're a Grand Old Flag"
   D. "This Land is Your Land"

2. Which of these is a favorite American frontiersman?
   A. Daniel Boone
   B. Martin Luther King, Jr.
   C. Rip Van Winkle
   D. Sacajawea

3. George W. Bush was the 43rd President of the United States. Who was the 42nd?
   A. George Bush
   B. Gerald Ford
   C. John Kennedy
   D. Bill Clinton

4. What is an abolitionist?
   A. a person from England who settled at Plymouth Rock
   B. a person who wanted to end slavery
   C. a person who leaves one country to live in another
   D. a person elected by people to represent them

5. Which of these states is the most visited by tourists?
   A. Arizona
   B. California
   C. Florida
   D. New York

6. Who wrote the famous "*I Have a Dream*" speech?
   A. Rev. Jesse Jackson
   B. General Colin Powell
   C. Martin Luther King, Jr.
   D. Malcolm X

Control your test anxiety by closing your eyes and taking two deep breaths.

Name: _____ Date: _____

Lesson One: History and Culture (cont.)

7. Which of these Native Americans was the principle guide for Lewis and Clark?
   A. Pochahontas
   B. Sacajawea
   C. Hiawatha
   D. Powhatan

8. Which of these characters from American folklore was supposedly raised by coyotes after he fell off a wagon train?
   A. Pecos Bill
   B. John Henry
   C. Paul Bunyan
   D. Johnny Appleseed

Don't panic! You aren't supposed to know *everything* on the test.

9. Which of these has become a symbol of freedom for oppressed people everywhere?
   A. Liberty Bell
   B. American Eagle
   C. Stars and Stripes
   D. Statue of Liberty

10. Who began the religion of Islam?
    A. Jesus Christ
    B. The Buddha
    C. Muhammad
    D. Abraham

11. What is the approximate population of the United States?
    A. almost 300 million people
    B. almost 3 million people
    C. almost a billion people
    D. more than a billion people

Benjamin Franklin

12. Who was Benjamin Franklin?
    A. the 3rd President of the United States
    B. a general during the Boston Massacre
    C. a colonial leader, printer, scientist, and writer
    D. the man who invented the bicycle

13. Who wrote a best-selling novel about the suffering of slaves prior to the Civil War?
    A. Harriet Tubman
    B. Sojourner Truth
    C. Harriet Beecher Stowe
    D. Dorothea Dix

Name: _____   Date: _____

Lesson One: History and Culture (cont.)

14. In 1954, the United States Supreme Court ruled <u>against</u>
    A. separate schools for black students and white students.
    B. school bussing.
    C. church bombings.
    D. affirmative action.

15. Who was the first person to walk on the moon?
    A. Sally Ride
    B. Buzz Aldrin
    C. Neil Armstrong
    D. John Glenn

Stay calm and focused. Don't let your mind wander.

16. The first African-American and the first woman to be the National Security Advisor was
    A. Oprah Winfrey.
    B. Rosa Parks.
    C. Condoleeza Rice.
    D. Barbara Jordan.

17. Which of these historical conflicts happened first?
    A. Civil War
    B. War of 1812
    C. Vietnam War
    D. World War II

18. Which of these inventions is the most recent?
    A. cotton gin
    B. automobile
    C. electric razor
    D. roller blades

20. A _____ is a person who makes a journey for religious reasons.
    A. colonist
    B. missionary
    C. pilgrim
    D. immigrant

19. What does the National Parks Service do?
    A. It protects the nation's national treasures.
    B. It collects fees for using national parks.
    C. It regulates the mining industry.
    D. It manages the nation's natural resources.

21. Which was the first town established by Europeans in the United States?
    A. Plymouth, Massachusetts
    B. St. Augustine, Florida
    C. Jamestown, Virginia
    D. Santa Fe, New Mexico

Name: _____   Date: _____

Lesson One: History and Culture (cont.)

Directions: Use Figures 1–3 about the original thirteen colonies to answer questions 22–27.

Figure 1

Colony	Year Founded	Founder	Reason for Founding
New York	1626	Dutch	to expand trade
A	1664	Lord John Berkeley, Sir George Carteret	religious and political freedom, investment
Pennsylvania	1681	**B**	religious and political freedom, investment
Delaware	1682	Dutch	to expand trade

Figure 2

Colony	Year Founded	Founder	Reason for Founding
Massachusetts	1620	**C**	religious freedom
New Hampshire	1623	the colonists who left Massachusetts	religious freedom, profit from trade
Rhode Island	1636	Roger Williams	religious freedom
Connecticut	1636	Thomas Hooker	religious and political freedom

Figure 3

Colony	Year Founded	Founder	Reason for Founding
Virginia	1607	John Smith	trade and agriculture
Maryland	1634	Lord Baltimore	**E**
North Carolina	1654	Virginia settlers	religious freedom, profit from trade and agriculture
South Carolina	1663	English	religious freedom, profit from trade and agriculture
Georgia	1732	**D**	haven for debtors, investment

Name: _____ Date: _____

Lesson One: History and Culture (cont.)

22. Which Figure lists the New England Colonies?
    A. 1
    B. 2
    C. 3
    D. none

Social Studies is about people, places, and events and how and why they happened.

23. What word/words belong in space **A**?
    A. Rhode Island
    B. North Carolina
    C. New Jersey
    D. Georgia

24. What name belongs in space **B**?
    A. Roger Willliams
    B. Lord Baltimore
    C. John Smith
    D. William Penn

25. Which belongs in space **C**?
    A. Pilgrims
    B. Colonists
    C. English
    D. Dutch

26. What name belongs in space **D**?
    A. Lord Baltimore
    B. John Smith
    C. James Oglethorpe
    D. Roger Williams

27. What belongs in space **E**?
    A. religious freedom
    B. political freedom
    C. expanded trade
    D. investment profit

28. Which of these historical events was the first to occur?
    A. The Declaration of Independence was signed.
    B. Boston Tea Party
    C. French and Indian War
    D. The Constitution was ratified.

Name: _____ Date: _____

Lesson One: History and Culture (cont.)

29. In 1838, the U.S. government forced the Cherokee to relocate to Oklahoma. What was this mass migration called?
    A.   The Trail of Tears
    B.   The Mississippi March
    C.   The Grand Canyon Advance
    D.   The Indian Retinue

30. Who was President of the United States during the Civil War?
    A.   George Washington
    B.   Ulysses S. Grant
    C.   Abraham Lincoln
    D.   Andrew Jackson

31. Who did the United States fight during World War II?
    A.   France and Spain
    B.   Russia and China
    C.   Germany and Japan
    D.   Canada and Mexico

32. Who was the first person to fly alone nonstop across the Atlantic Ocean?
    A.   John Glenn
    B.   Wright Brothers
    C.   Charles Lindbergh
    D.   Chuck Yeager

33. Put the U.S. conflicts listed on the right in chronological order.
    A.   1, 2, 3, 4
    B.   2, 1, 4, 3
    C.   3, 4, 1, 2
    D.   2, 3, 4,1

1.	Korean War
2.	World War II
3.	Gulf War
4.	Vietnam War

Read and consider all answer choices. Don't be tricked into choosing too quickly.

34. Why was Richard Nixon forced to resign as President?
    A.   because of the Watergate scandal
    B.   because of the Teapot Dome scandal
    C.   because of the Monica Lewinsky scandal
    D.   because of the White Water scandal

35. The ancient Chinese people invented all but which one?
    A.   paper
    B.   gunpowder
    C.   acupuncture
    D.   wheel

Name: _____   Date: _____

Lesson One: History and Culture (cont.)

36. All but which one are achievements of the early Greeks?
    A. great architecture
    B. great poets
    C. great aqueducts
    D. great thinkers

37. The Romans contributed all but which one of these?
    A. great music
    B. great writers
    C. great roads
    D. great sculpture

38. Who did the United States fight in the "Cold War"?
    A. France
    B. Japan
    C. Soviet Union
    D. Iran

39. In 2001, the United States military overthrew the Taliban regime in which country?
    A. Iran
    B. Afghanistan
    C. Iraq
    D. Pakistan

40. In 2003, the United States military overthrew the government of Saddam Hussein in which country?
    A. Iran
    B. Afghanistan
    C. Iraq
    D. Pakistan

Review

1. Control your test anxiety by closing your eyes and taking two deep breaths.

2. Don't panic! You're not supposed to know *everything* on the test.

3. Stay calm and focused. Don't let your mind wander.

4. Social studies is about people, places, and events and how and why they happened.

5. Read and consider all answer choices. Don't be tricked into choosing too soon.

Name: _____ Date: _____

UNIT FIVE: SOCIAL STUDIES

Lesson Two: Civics, Government, and Economics

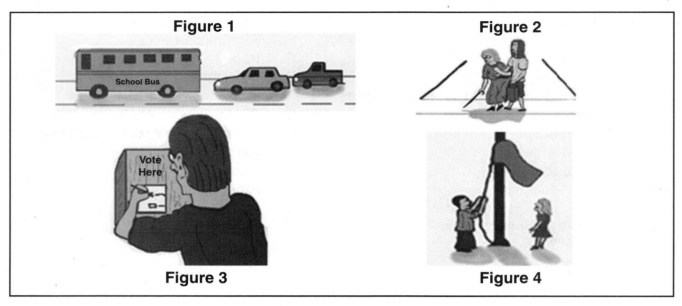

Figure 1   Figure 2

School Bus

Vote Here

Figure 3   Figure 4

1. Which of the above pictures shows good citizenship?
   A. 1 and 2
   B. 2 and 3
   C. 1 and 4
   D. all of them

2. Which one of the following examples shows good citizenship?
   A. rewinding rented movies
   B. playing baseball with a friend
   C. cheating on a test
   D. making fun of an elderly neighbor

3. Which is the correct order for these important documents?
   A. Articles of Confederation, Constitution, Declaration of Independence, Bill of Rights
   B. Bill of Rights, Constitution, Articles of Confederation, Declaration of Independence
   C. Declaration of Independence, Articles of Confederation, Constitution, Bill of Rights
   D. Declaration of Independence, Constitution, Articles of Confederation, Bill of Rights

4. Which document declared "that all persons held as slaves are, and henceforth, shall be free"?
   A. Bill of Rights
   B. Emancipation Proclamation
   C. Gettysburg Address
   D. Articles of Confederation

Name: _____ Date: _____

Lesson Two: Civics, Government, and Economics (cont.)

5. "We hold these truths to be self-evident, that all men are created equal ..." is from which important U.S. document?
   - A.   Bill of Rights
   - B.   Constitution
   - C.   Declaration of Independence
   - D.   Articles of Confederation

Social studies tests usually include questions about history, geography, cultures, and government.

6. What is an *amendment*?
   - A.   a bill that has passed Congress
   - B.   a proposal to alter the provisions of the Constitution
   - C.   traffic in goods traded between states
   - D.   a union of states

7. The first ten amendments to the U.S. Constitution are called
   - A.   the Freedom Amendments.
   - B.   the Articles of Confederation.
   - C.   the Citizenship Laws.
   - D.   the Bill of Rights.

8. What is meant by the *separation of powers*?
   - A.   the distribution of power and authority among the legislative, executive, and judicial branches of government
   - B.   The three branches of government must remain separate from each other.
   - C.   None of the three branches of government may interfere with the work of the other two.
   - D.   State governments must remain separate from the federal government.

Sometimes you can figure out an answer for an earlier question from one that comes later. Look at #7. Does it give you an idea of the answer for #6?

Name: _____   Date: _____

Lesson Two: Civics, Government, and Economics (cont.)

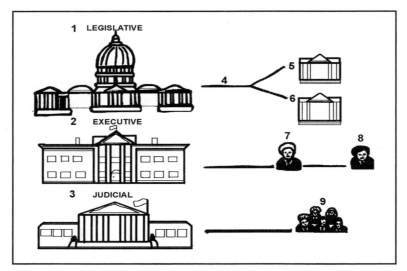

Figure 5: The Branches of Government

9.   What is the name of the building that houses the legislative branch (#1)?
     A.   the White House
     B.   the U.S. Capitol Building
     C.   the Federal Office Building
     D.   the Supreme Court

10. Which group in Figure 5 includes the Chief Justice of the Supreme Court?
     A. 5   B. 6   C. 7   D. 9

11. Which branch of the government is responsible for deciding if a law or government action violates the Constitution?
     A. 1   B. 2   C. 3   D. 7

12. Where on the diagram does the Congress go?
     A. 3   B. 4   C. 5   D. 6

13. Which branch has the authority to make laws?
     A. 1   B. 2   C. 3   D. 9

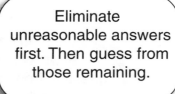

Eliminate unreasonable answers first. Then guess from those remaining.

14. Congress is divided into two bodies (#5 and #6). Which one of these is composed of two representatives from each state?
     A.   the Supreme Court
     B.   the Executive Branch
     C.   the House of Representatives
     D.   the Senate

Name: _____ Date: _____

Lesson Two: Civics, Government, and Economics (cont.)

15. #7 represents the head of the Executive Branch. Who is it?
    A. the President
    B. the Vice President
    C. the Supreme Court
    D. the Congress

16. What building is represented in #2?
    A. the United States Capitol Building
    B. the White House
    C. the Supreme Court
    D. the Smithsonian

17. What is the purpose of the system of *checks and balances*?
    A. to keep each of the three branches separate but equal
    B. to have a group who can veto proposed legislation
    C. to keep any one branch from getting too powerful
    D. to have someone responsible for collecting tax money

18. *President* is to *United States* as _____ is to a *state*.
    A. senator
    B. governor
    C. mayor
    D. police person

Always read all answer choices.

19. Why do citizens have to pay taxes?
    A. to pay for the government
    B. to pay for public schools
    C. to pay for the services the government provides
    D. to pay the President's salary

20. Why is the United States often called a "nation of immigrants"?
    A. The United States has a diverse population.
    B. Many people left their native lands to live in the United States.
    C. People have different customs.
    D. All of the above

21. What is a *naturalized citizen*?
    A. a citizen born to a U.S. citizen
    B. a citizen born outside the U.S. who was granted citizenship
    C. a citizen with a green card
    D. a citizen who works outside the United States

Name: _____ Date: _____

Lesson Two: Civics, Government, and Economics (cont.)

22. What is the purpose of the President's Cabinet?
    A.   to make decisions for the President
    B.   to take over if the President is ill
    C.   to advise the President
    D.   to keep the President from making mistakes

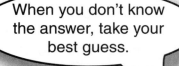

When you don't know the answer, take your best guess.

23. What does the Secretary of State do?
    A.   takes notes in Cabinet meetings
    B.   handles foreign affairs and relationships with other nations
    C.   protects our country from terrorist attacks
    D.   handles education matters

24. Which one of the following departments is responsible for protecting America from terrorist attacks?
    A.   Department of Homeland Security
    B.   Department of Defense
    C.   Department of Health and Human Services
    D.   Department of Justice

25. Who is commander-in-chief of the U.S. military?
    A.   the Secretary of Defense
    B.   the Attorney General
    C.   the President
    D.   the Secretary of State

26. All but which one of these is a reason to save money?
    A.   to purchase something in the future that you decide you want
    B.   to make a lot of money in interest
    C.   to buy something you suddenly see and want
    D.   to deal with emergencies and unexpected events

27. Goods and services produced by the government are called *public goods*. Which of the following is a public good?
    A.   grocery store
    B.   computer company
    C.   public school
    D.   pizza restaurant

28. What is *inflation*?
    A.   a period of generally rising prices
    B.   something that promotes or enhances well-being
    C.   a schedule showing amounts of a good or service
    D.   a period of generally declining prices

Name: _____ Date: _____

Lesson Two: Civics, Government, and Economics (cont.)

29. What do people do at the Stock Exchange?
    A. exchange company stock with others
    B. run around throwing paper in the air
    C. shout the cost of companies to one another
    D. buy and sell shares of stock in companies

30. What is a *depression*?
    A. a severe mood swing
    B. a period of severe drought
    C. a severe business slowdown
    D. a period of severe goods shortages

Price History - XYZ (12/9/01-12/8/2002)

Name	Last	Change	% Chg
Dow	10,145.26 ▲ +15.70		+0.16%
S&P	1,076.48 ▲ +1.35		+0.13%
NASDAQ	1,921.33 ▼ -2.96		-.015%

Review

1. Social Studies tests usually include questions about history, geography, cultures, and government.

2. Sometimes you can figure out an answer for an earlier question from one that comes later.

3. Eliminate unreasonable answers first. Then guess from those remaining.

4. <u>Always</u> read all answer choices.

5. When you don't know the answer, take your best guess.

Name: _____ Date: _____

UNIT FIVE: SOCIAL STUDIES

Lesson Three: Geography

Directions: Use Figure 1 to answer questions 1–3.

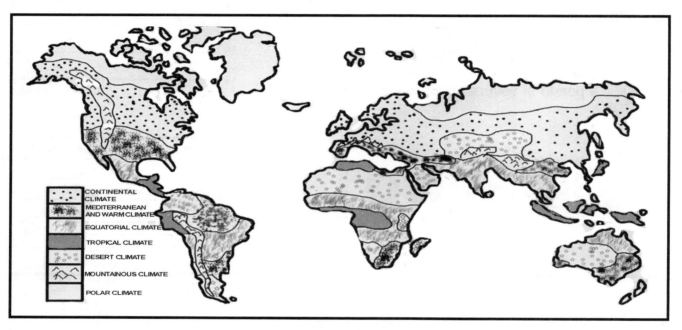

Figure 1

1. Which of these weather forecasts for the month of September would be most accurate?
   A. London: tropical breezes and monsoon rains
   B. Mexico City: ice storms will continue.
   C. Cairo, Egypt: temperatures over 100, no rain in sight
   D. Sydney, Australia: snow showers with accumulation up to 2 feet

2. What is the climate of Greenland?
   A. Continental climate
   B. Polar climate
   C. Tropical climate
   D. Equatorial climate

3. All but which one of these affects climate?
   A. latitude
   B. elevation
   C. large bodies of water
   D. volcanoes

Use common sense when choosing an answer.

Name: _____   Date: _____

Lesson Three: Geography (cont.)

Directions: Use Figure 2 to answer questions 4–7.

4. From Fish Haven, in what direction are the Lava Hot Springs?
   A. south
   B. east
   C. north
   D. west

5. Which route would be quickest to get from Virginia to Soda Springs?
   A. 91
   B. 15
   C. 30
   D. 34

6. On this map, the Oregon Trail goes through which two states?
   A. Idaho and Wyoming
   B. Wyoming and Utah
   C. Utah and Nevada
   D. Utah and Wyoming

7. Which town is on the Bear River?
   A. Georgetown
   B. Mink Creek
   C. Henry
   D. Bear Lake

8. The United States shares its longest border with
   A. Michigan.
   B. Wyoming.
   C. Canada.
   D. Mexico.

9. Which of these is <u>not</u> a Pacific Coast state?
   A. Oregon
   B. Washington
   C. California
   D. Arizona

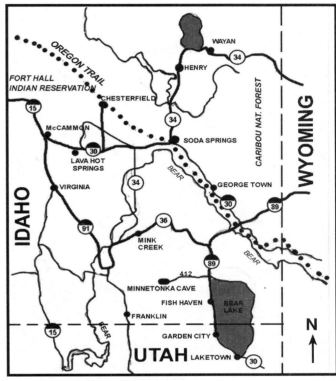

Figure 2

Study maps carefully before attempting to answer the questions.

Name: _____ Date: _____

Lesson Three: Geography (cont.)

10. The Rocky Mountains are in all but which one of these states?
    A.   South Dakota
    B.   Colorado
    C.   Wyoming
    D.   Idaho

11. What is the capital of Kansas?
    A.   Springfield
    B.   Topeka
    C.   Kansas City
    D.   Wichita

> Make sure that you understand the question.

12. All but which one of the Great Lakes touches Michigan?
    A.   Lake Erie
    B.   Lake Huron
    C.   Lake Superior
    D.   Lake Ontario

13. Which of these is not true?
    A.   Tennessee is north of Alabama
    B.   Colorado is west of Utah
    C.   Montana is east of Idaho
    D.   Louisiana is south of Mississippi

14. Which of these countries in North America is noted for its size, its two official languages, its north magnetic pole, and its open border?
    A.   United States
    B.   Mexico
    C.   Canada
    D.   Cuba

15. Which of these countries in North America has the largest population?
    A.   United States
    B.   Mexico
    C.   Canada
    D.   Cuba

16. What is a canal?
    A.   a long hill of dirt or stone built to turn back floodwaters
    B.   a waterway made by people so boats can transport goods
    C.   a mass of ice that moves very slowly
    D.   a piece of land that sticks out into the water

Name: _____ Date: _____

Lesson Three: Geography (cont.)

17. Which of these does not belong?
    A. Sacramento
    B. San Francisco
    C. Denver
    D. Los Angeles

18. Which of these does not belong?
    A. Pittsburgh
    B. Chicago
    C. New Orleans
    D. Toronto

Don't change an answer unless you are <u>really</u> sure.

19. Which of these does not belong?
    A. Amazon
    B. Mississippi
    C. Yukon
    D. Rio Grande

20. What is the largest continent in the world?
    A. North America
    B. Asia
    C. Antarctica
    D. South America

21. The largest ocean in the world is the
    A. Atlantic.
    B. Indian.
    C. Arctic.
    D. Pacific.

22. The world's largest desert is the Sahara. Where is it located?
    A. Africa
    B. North America
    C. Asia
    D. South America

23. What is the largest state in the United States?
    A. Texas
    B. California
    C. Alaska
    D. Florida

Name: _____ Date: _____

Lesson Three: Geography (cont.)

24. The Northern and Southern Hemispheres are divided by the
    A. Prime Meridian.
    B. equator.
    C. water.
    D. longitude.

25. What separates the Eastern and Western Hemispheres?
    A. Prime Meridian
    B. equator
    C. water
    D. latitude

Don't worry if others finish while you are still working.

Directions: Use Figure 3 to answer questions 26–28.

---

26. If it is 1:00 P.M. in Chicago, what time is it in Los Angeles?
    A. 10:00 A.M.
    B. 11:00 A.M.
    C. 3:00 P.M.
    D. 2:00 P.M.

27. If it is noon in Hawaii, what time is it in New York?
    A. 8:00 A.M.
    B. 10:00 A.M.
    C. 3:00 P.M.
    D. 5:00 P.M.

28. Why is the time later on the east coast than on the west coast?
    A. Someone ordered it this way.
    B. It's just a custom to tell time this way.
    C. The sun appears to rise in the east and set in the west.
    D. daylight saving time

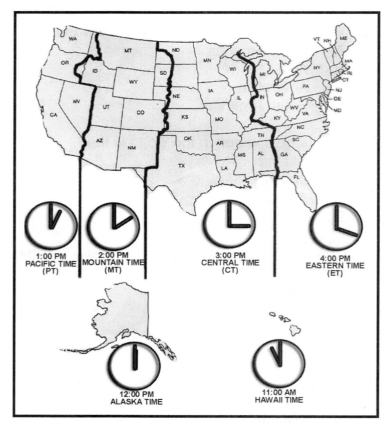

Figure 3

Name: _____ Date: _____

Lesson Three: Geography (cont.)

29. The city in the United States with the greatest population is
    A. New York.
    B. Los Angeles.
    C. Chicago.
    D. Houston.

Remember that a test is not a race!

30. The state with the most area of tribal land is
    A. New York.
    B. Arizona.
    C. Ohio.
    D. Florida.

Directions: Use Figure 4 to answer questions 31–35.

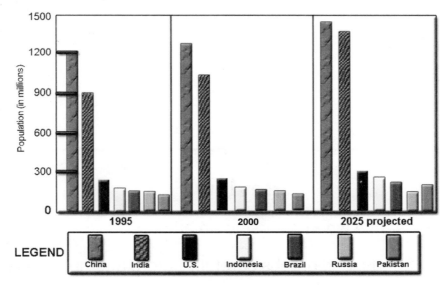

Figure 4

31. What is the projected population of Pakistan in 2025?
    A. over 300 million
    B. approximately 900 million people
    C. about 240 million
    D. over 150 million

32. All but which one of these countries is projected to grow by over 100 million from 1995 to 2025?
    A. China   C. Indonesia
    B. India   D. Russia

Name: _____   Date: _____

Lesson Three: Geography (cont.)

33. Which country has the greatest projected growth
    from 2000 to 2025?
    A.   India
    B.   China
    C.   Pakistan
    D.   Indonesia

34. Which two countries are likely to have over
    1 billion people by 2025?
    A.   India and Pakistan
    B.   China and the United States
    C.   the United States and Russia
    D.   India and China

35. What will the approximate population of the
    United States be in 2025?
    A.   150,000,000
    B.   900,000,000
    C.   300,000,000
    D.   500,000,000

> Later questions
> may provide answers
> or clues to answers
> earlier on the test.
> Pay attention!

Review

1. Use common sense when choosing an answer.

2. Study maps, charts, and graphs carefully before attempting to answer
   a question.

3. Make sure that you understand the question.

4. Don't change an answer unless you are <u>really</u> sure.

5. Don't worry if others finish while you are still working.

6. Remember that taking a test is not a race!

7. Later questions may provide answers or clues to answers earlier on
   the test. Pay attention!

104

Name: _____ Date: _____

Standardized Testing Answer Sheet

School:	Student Name			
Teacher:	Last		First	MI

Female ○   Male ○

Birth Date		
Month	Day	Year

Jan ○	⓪ ⓪	⓪ ⓪
Feb ○	① ①	① ①
Mar ○	② ②	② ②
Apr ○	③ ③	③ ③
May ○	④	④ ④
Jun ○	⑤	⑤ ⑤
Jul ○	⑥	⑥ ⑥
Aug ○	⑦	⑦ ⑦
Sep ○	⑧	⑧ ⑧
Oct ○	⑨	⑨ ⑨
Nov ○		
Dec ○		

Grade
③
④
⑤
⑥
⑦
⑧

(Student name grid with circles and letters A–Z for each column)

Unit One: Reading   Lesson One: Vocabulary

1. Ⓐ Ⓑ Ⓒ Ⓓ   10. Ⓐ Ⓑ Ⓒ Ⓓ   19. Ⓐ Ⓑ Ⓒ Ⓓ   28. Ⓐ Ⓑ Ⓒ Ⓓ   37. Ⓐ Ⓑ Ⓒ Ⓓ
2. Ⓐ Ⓑ Ⓒ Ⓓ   11. Ⓐ Ⓑ Ⓒ Ⓓ   20. Ⓐ Ⓑ Ⓒ Ⓓ   29. Ⓐ Ⓑ Ⓒ Ⓓ   38. Ⓐ Ⓑ Ⓒ Ⓓ
3. Ⓐ Ⓑ Ⓒ Ⓓ   12. Ⓐ Ⓑ Ⓒ Ⓓ   21. Ⓐ Ⓑ Ⓒ Ⓓ   30. Ⓐ Ⓑ Ⓒ Ⓓ   39. Ⓐ Ⓑ Ⓒ Ⓓ
4. Ⓐ Ⓑ Ⓒ Ⓓ   13. Ⓐ Ⓑ Ⓒ Ⓓ   22. Ⓐ Ⓑ Ⓒ Ⓓ   31. Ⓐ Ⓑ Ⓒ Ⓓ   40. Ⓐ Ⓑ Ⓒ Ⓓ
5. Ⓐ Ⓑ Ⓒ Ⓓ   14. Ⓐ Ⓑ Ⓒ Ⓓ   23. Ⓐ Ⓑ Ⓒ Ⓓ   32. Ⓐ Ⓑ Ⓒ Ⓓ   41. Ⓐ Ⓑ Ⓒ Ⓓ
6. Ⓐ Ⓑ Ⓒ Ⓓ   15. Ⓐ Ⓑ Ⓒ Ⓓ   24. Ⓐ Ⓑ Ⓒ Ⓓ   33. Ⓐ Ⓑ Ⓒ Ⓓ   42. Ⓐ Ⓑ Ⓒ Ⓓ
7. Ⓐ Ⓑ Ⓒ Ⓓ   16. Ⓐ Ⓑ Ⓒ Ⓓ   25. Ⓐ Ⓑ Ⓒ Ⓓ   34. Ⓐ Ⓑ Ⓒ Ⓓ   43. Ⓐ Ⓑ Ⓒ Ⓓ
8. Ⓐ Ⓑ Ⓒ Ⓓ   17. Ⓐ Ⓑ Ⓒ Ⓓ   26. Ⓐ Ⓑ Ⓒ Ⓓ   35. Ⓐ Ⓑ Ⓒ Ⓓ   44. Ⓐ Ⓑ Ⓒ Ⓓ
9. Ⓐ Ⓑ Ⓒ Ⓓ   18. Ⓐ Ⓑ Ⓒ Ⓓ   27. Ⓐ Ⓑ Ⓒ Ⓓ   36. Ⓐ Ⓑ Ⓒ Ⓓ   45. Ⓐ Ⓑ Ⓒ Ⓓ

Name: _____ Date: _____

Standardized Testing   Answer Sheet

Unit One: Reading   **Lesson Two: Word Analysis**

1. Ⓐ Ⓑ Ⓒ Ⓓ   13. Ⓐ Ⓑ Ⓒ Ⓓ   25. Ⓐ Ⓑ Ⓒ Ⓓ   37. Ⓐ Ⓑ Ⓒ Ⓓ   49. Ⓐ Ⓑ Ⓒ Ⓓ
2. Ⓐ Ⓑ Ⓒ Ⓓ   14. Ⓐ Ⓑ Ⓒ Ⓓ   26. Ⓐ Ⓑ Ⓒ Ⓓ   38. Ⓐ Ⓑ Ⓒ Ⓓ   50. Ⓐ Ⓑ Ⓒ Ⓓ
3. Ⓐ Ⓑ Ⓒ Ⓓ   15. Ⓐ Ⓑ Ⓒ Ⓓ   27. Ⓐ Ⓑ Ⓒ Ⓓ   39. Ⓐ Ⓑ Ⓒ Ⓓ   51. Ⓐ Ⓑ Ⓒ Ⓓ
4. Ⓐ Ⓑ Ⓒ Ⓓ   16. Ⓐ Ⓑ Ⓒ Ⓓ   28. Ⓐ Ⓑ Ⓒ Ⓓ   40. Ⓐ Ⓑ Ⓒ Ⓓ   52. Ⓐ Ⓑ Ⓒ Ⓓ
5. Ⓐ Ⓑ Ⓒ Ⓓ   17. Ⓐ Ⓑ Ⓒ Ⓓ   29. Ⓐ Ⓑ Ⓒ Ⓓ   41. Ⓐ Ⓑ Ⓒ Ⓓ   53. Ⓐ Ⓑ Ⓒ Ⓓ
6. Ⓐ Ⓑ Ⓒ Ⓓ   18. Ⓐ Ⓑ Ⓒ Ⓓ   30. Ⓐ Ⓑ Ⓒ Ⓓ   42. Ⓐ Ⓑ Ⓒ Ⓓ   54. Ⓐ Ⓑ Ⓒ Ⓓ
7. Ⓐ Ⓑ Ⓒ Ⓓ   19. Ⓐ Ⓑ Ⓒ Ⓓ   31. Ⓐ Ⓑ Ⓒ Ⓓ   43. Ⓐ Ⓑ Ⓒ Ⓓ   55. Ⓐ Ⓑ Ⓒ Ⓓ
8. Ⓐ Ⓑ Ⓒ Ⓓ   20. Ⓐ Ⓑ Ⓒ Ⓓ   32. Ⓐ Ⓑ Ⓒ Ⓓ   44. Ⓐ Ⓑ Ⓒ Ⓓ   56. Ⓐ Ⓑ Ⓒ Ⓓ
9. Ⓐ Ⓑ Ⓒ Ⓓ   21. Ⓐ Ⓑ Ⓒ Ⓓ   33. Ⓐ Ⓑ Ⓒ Ⓓ   45. Ⓐ Ⓑ Ⓒ Ⓓ   57. Ⓐ Ⓑ Ⓒ Ⓓ
10. Ⓐ Ⓑ Ⓒ Ⓓ   22. Ⓐ Ⓑ Ⓒ Ⓓ   34. Ⓐ Ⓑ Ⓒ Ⓓ   46. Ⓐ Ⓑ Ⓒ Ⓓ   58. Ⓐ Ⓑ Ⓒ Ⓓ
11. Ⓐ Ⓑ Ⓒ Ⓓ   23. Ⓐ Ⓑ Ⓒ Ⓓ   35. Ⓐ Ⓑ Ⓒ Ⓓ   47. Ⓐ Ⓑ Ⓒ Ⓓ   59. Ⓐ Ⓑ Ⓒ Ⓓ
12. Ⓐ Ⓑ Ⓒ Ⓓ   24. Ⓐ Ⓑ Ⓒ Ⓓ   36. Ⓐ Ⓑ Ⓒ Ⓓ   48. Ⓐ Ⓑ Ⓒ Ⓓ   60. Ⓐ Ⓑ Ⓒ Ⓓ

Unit One: Reading   **Lesson Three: Comprehension**

1. Ⓐ Ⓑ Ⓒ Ⓓ   11. Ⓐ Ⓑ Ⓒ Ⓓ   21. Ⓐ Ⓑ Ⓒ Ⓓ   31. Ⓐ Ⓑ Ⓒ Ⓓ   41. Ⓐ Ⓑ Ⓒ Ⓓ
2. Ⓐ Ⓑ Ⓒ Ⓓ   12. Ⓐ Ⓑ Ⓒ Ⓓ   22. Ⓐ Ⓑ Ⓒ Ⓓ   32. Ⓐ Ⓑ Ⓒ Ⓓ   42. Ⓐ Ⓑ Ⓒ Ⓓ
3. Ⓐ Ⓑ Ⓒ Ⓓ   13. Ⓐ Ⓑ Ⓒ Ⓓ   23. Ⓐ Ⓑ Ⓒ Ⓓ   33. Ⓐ Ⓑ Ⓒ Ⓓ   43. Ⓐ Ⓑ Ⓒ Ⓓ
4. Ⓐ Ⓑ Ⓒ Ⓓ   14. Ⓐ Ⓑ Ⓒ Ⓓ   24. Ⓐ Ⓑ Ⓒ Ⓓ   34. Ⓐ Ⓑ Ⓒ Ⓓ   44. Ⓐ Ⓑ Ⓒ Ⓓ
5. Ⓐ Ⓑ Ⓒ Ⓓ   15. Ⓐ Ⓑ Ⓒ Ⓓ   25. Ⓐ Ⓑ Ⓒ Ⓓ   35. Ⓐ Ⓑ Ⓒ Ⓓ   45. Ⓐ Ⓑ Ⓒ Ⓓ
6. Ⓐ Ⓑ Ⓒ Ⓓ   16. Ⓐ Ⓑ Ⓒ Ⓓ   26. Ⓐ Ⓑ Ⓒ Ⓓ   36. Ⓐ Ⓑ Ⓒ Ⓓ   46. Ⓐ Ⓑ Ⓒ Ⓓ
7. Ⓐ Ⓑ Ⓒ Ⓓ   17. Ⓐ Ⓑ Ⓒ Ⓓ   27. Ⓐ Ⓑ Ⓒ Ⓓ   37. Ⓐ Ⓑ Ⓒ Ⓓ   47. Ⓐ Ⓑ Ⓒ Ⓓ
8. Ⓐ Ⓑ Ⓒ Ⓓ   18. Ⓐ Ⓑ Ⓒ Ⓓ   28. Ⓐ Ⓑ Ⓒ Ⓓ   38. Ⓐ Ⓑ Ⓒ Ⓓ   48. Ⓐ Ⓑ Ⓒ Ⓓ
9. Ⓐ Ⓑ Ⓒ Ⓓ   19. Ⓐ Ⓑ Ⓒ Ⓓ   29. Ⓐ Ⓑ Ⓒ Ⓓ   39. Ⓐ Ⓑ Ⓒ Ⓓ   49. Ⓐ Ⓑ Ⓒ Ⓓ
10. Ⓐ Ⓑ Ⓒ Ⓓ   20. Ⓐ Ⓑ Ⓒ Ⓓ   30. Ⓐ Ⓑ Ⓒ Ⓓ   40. Ⓐ Ⓑ Ⓒ Ⓓ   50. Ⓐ Ⓑ Ⓒ Ⓓ

Unit Two: Language   **Lesson One: Mechanics**

1. Ⓐ Ⓑ Ⓒ Ⓓ   8. Ⓐ Ⓑ Ⓒ Ⓓ   15. Ⓐ Ⓑ Ⓒ Ⓓ   22. Ⓐ Ⓑ Ⓒ Ⓓ   29. Ⓐ Ⓑ Ⓒ Ⓓ
2. Ⓐ Ⓑ Ⓒ Ⓓ   9. Ⓐ Ⓑ Ⓒ Ⓓ   16. Ⓐ Ⓑ Ⓒ Ⓓ   23. Ⓐ Ⓑ Ⓒ Ⓓ   30. Ⓐ Ⓑ Ⓒ Ⓓ
3. Ⓐ Ⓑ Ⓒ Ⓓ   10. Ⓐ Ⓑ Ⓒ Ⓓ   17. Ⓐ Ⓑ Ⓒ Ⓓ   24. Ⓐ Ⓑ Ⓒ Ⓓ   31. Ⓐ Ⓑ Ⓒ Ⓓ
4. Ⓐ Ⓑ Ⓒ Ⓓ   11. Ⓐ Ⓑ Ⓒ Ⓓ   18. Ⓐ Ⓑ Ⓒ Ⓓ   25. Ⓐ Ⓑ Ⓒ Ⓓ   32. Ⓐ Ⓑ Ⓒ Ⓓ
5. Ⓐ Ⓑ Ⓒ Ⓓ   12. Ⓐ Ⓑ Ⓒ Ⓓ   19. Ⓐ Ⓑ Ⓒ Ⓓ   26. Ⓐ Ⓑ Ⓒ Ⓓ   33. Ⓐ Ⓑ Ⓒ Ⓓ
6. Ⓐ Ⓑ Ⓒ Ⓓ   13. Ⓐ Ⓑ Ⓒ Ⓓ   20. Ⓐ Ⓑ Ⓒ Ⓓ   27. Ⓐ Ⓑ Ⓒ Ⓓ   34. Ⓐ Ⓑ Ⓒ Ⓓ
7. Ⓐ Ⓑ Ⓒ Ⓓ   14. Ⓐ Ⓑ Ⓒ Ⓓ   21. Ⓐ Ⓑ Ⓒ Ⓓ   28. Ⓐ Ⓑ Ⓒ Ⓓ   35. Ⓐ Ⓑ Ⓒ Ⓓ

Standardized Testing ___ Answer Sheet

Unit Two: Language   Lesson Two: Expression

1. Ⓐ Ⓑ Ⓒ Ⓓ   6. Ⓐ Ⓑ Ⓒ Ⓓ   11. Ⓐ Ⓑ Ⓒ Ⓓ   16. Ⓐ Ⓑ Ⓒ Ⓓ   21. Ⓐ Ⓑ Ⓒ Ⓓ
2. Ⓐ Ⓑ Ⓒ Ⓓ   7. Ⓐ Ⓑ Ⓒ Ⓓ   12. Ⓐ Ⓑ Ⓒ Ⓓ   17. Ⓐ Ⓑ Ⓒ Ⓓ   22. Ⓐ Ⓑ Ⓒ Ⓓ
3. Ⓐ Ⓑ Ⓒ Ⓓ   8. Ⓐ Ⓑ Ⓒ Ⓓ   13. Ⓐ Ⓑ Ⓒ Ⓓ   18. Ⓐ Ⓑ Ⓒ Ⓓ   23. Ⓐ Ⓑ Ⓒ Ⓓ
4. Ⓐ Ⓑ Ⓒ Ⓓ   9. Ⓐ Ⓑ Ⓒ Ⓓ   14. Ⓐ Ⓑ Ⓒ Ⓓ   19. Ⓐ Ⓑ Ⓒ Ⓓ   24. Ⓐ Ⓑ Ⓒ Ⓓ
5. Ⓐ Ⓑ Ⓒ Ⓓ   10. Ⓐ Ⓑ Ⓒ Ⓓ   15. Ⓐ Ⓑ Ⓒ Ⓓ   20. Ⓐ Ⓑ Ⓒ Ⓓ   25. Ⓐ Ⓑ Ⓒ Ⓓ

Unit Two: Language   Lesson Three: Information Skills

1. Ⓐ Ⓑ Ⓒ Ⓓ   7. Ⓐ Ⓑ Ⓒ Ⓓ   13. Ⓐ Ⓑ Ⓒ Ⓓ   19. Ⓐ Ⓑ Ⓒ Ⓓ   25. Ⓐ Ⓑ Ⓒ Ⓓ
2. Ⓐ Ⓑ Ⓒ Ⓓ   8. Ⓐ Ⓑ Ⓒ Ⓓ   14. Ⓐ Ⓑ Ⓒ Ⓓ   20. Ⓐ Ⓑ Ⓒ Ⓓ   26. Ⓐ Ⓑ Ⓒ Ⓓ
3. Ⓐ Ⓑ Ⓒ Ⓓ   9. Ⓐ Ⓑ Ⓒ Ⓓ   15. Ⓐ Ⓑ Ⓒ Ⓓ   21. Ⓐ Ⓑ Ⓒ Ⓓ   27. Ⓐ Ⓑ Ⓒ Ⓓ
4. Ⓐ Ⓑ Ⓒ Ⓓ   10. Ⓐ Ⓑ Ⓒ Ⓓ   16. Ⓐ Ⓑ Ⓒ Ⓓ   22. Ⓐ Ⓑ Ⓒ Ⓓ   28. Ⓐ Ⓑ Ⓒ Ⓓ
5. Ⓐ Ⓑ Ⓒ Ⓓ   11. Ⓐ Ⓑ Ⓒ Ⓓ   17. Ⓐ Ⓑ Ⓒ Ⓓ   23. Ⓐ Ⓑ Ⓒ Ⓓ   29. Ⓐ Ⓑ Ⓒ Ⓓ
6. Ⓐ Ⓑ Ⓒ Ⓓ   12. Ⓐ Ⓑ Ⓒ Ⓓ   18. Ⓐ Ⓑ Ⓒ Ⓓ   24. Ⓐ Ⓑ Ⓒ Ⓓ   30. Ⓐ Ⓑ Ⓒ Ⓓ

Unit Three: Mathematics   Lesson One: Concepts

1. Ⓐ Ⓑ Ⓒ Ⓓ   11. Ⓐ Ⓑ Ⓒ Ⓓ   21. Ⓐ Ⓑ Ⓒ Ⓓ   31. Ⓐ Ⓑ Ⓒ Ⓓ   41. Ⓐ Ⓑ Ⓒ Ⓓ
2. Ⓐ Ⓑ Ⓒ Ⓓ   12. Ⓐ Ⓑ Ⓒ Ⓓ   22. Ⓐ Ⓑ Ⓒ Ⓓ   32. Ⓐ Ⓑ Ⓒ Ⓓ   42. Ⓐ Ⓑ Ⓒ Ⓓ
3. Ⓐ Ⓑ Ⓒ Ⓓ   13. Ⓐ Ⓑ Ⓒ Ⓓ   23. Ⓐ Ⓑ Ⓒ Ⓓ   33. Ⓐ Ⓑ Ⓒ Ⓓ   43. Ⓐ Ⓑ Ⓒ Ⓓ
4. Ⓐ Ⓑ Ⓒ Ⓓ   14. Ⓐ Ⓑ Ⓒ Ⓓ   24. Ⓐ Ⓑ Ⓒ Ⓓ   34. Ⓐ Ⓑ Ⓒ Ⓓ   44. Ⓐ Ⓑ Ⓒ Ⓓ
5. Ⓐ Ⓑ Ⓒ Ⓓ   15. Ⓐ Ⓑ Ⓒ Ⓓ   25. Ⓐ Ⓑ Ⓒ Ⓓ   35. Ⓐ Ⓑ Ⓒ Ⓓ   45. Ⓐ Ⓑ Ⓒ Ⓓ
6. Ⓐ Ⓑ Ⓒ Ⓓ   16. Ⓐ Ⓑ Ⓒ Ⓓ   26. Ⓐ Ⓑ Ⓒ Ⓓ   36. Ⓐ Ⓑ Ⓒ Ⓓ   46. Ⓐ Ⓑ Ⓒ Ⓓ
7. Ⓐ Ⓑ Ⓒ Ⓓ   17. Ⓐ Ⓑ Ⓒ Ⓓ   27. Ⓐ Ⓑ Ⓒ Ⓓ   37. Ⓐ Ⓑ Ⓒ Ⓓ   47. Ⓐ Ⓑ Ⓒ Ⓓ
8. Ⓐ Ⓑ Ⓒ Ⓓ   18. Ⓐ Ⓑ Ⓒ Ⓓ   28. Ⓐ Ⓑ Ⓒ Ⓓ   38. Ⓐ Ⓑ Ⓒ Ⓓ   48. Ⓐ Ⓑ Ⓒ Ⓓ
9. Ⓐ Ⓑ Ⓒ Ⓓ   19. Ⓐ Ⓑ Ⓒ Ⓓ   29. Ⓐ Ⓑ Ⓒ Ⓓ   39. Ⓐ Ⓑ Ⓒ Ⓓ   49. Ⓐ Ⓑ Ⓒ Ⓓ
10. Ⓐ Ⓑ Ⓒ Ⓓ   20. Ⓐ Ⓑ Ⓒ Ⓓ   30. Ⓐ Ⓑ Ⓒ Ⓓ   40. Ⓐ Ⓑ Ⓒ Ⓓ   50. Ⓐ Ⓑ Ⓒ Ⓓ

Unit Three: Mathematics   Lesson Two: Computation

1. Ⓐ Ⓑ Ⓒ Ⓓ   7. Ⓐ Ⓑ Ⓒ Ⓓ   13. Ⓐ Ⓑ Ⓒ Ⓓ   19. Ⓐ Ⓑ Ⓒ Ⓓ   25. Ⓐ Ⓑ Ⓒ Ⓓ
2. Ⓐ Ⓑ Ⓒ Ⓓ   8. Ⓐ Ⓑ Ⓒ Ⓓ   14. Ⓐ Ⓑ Ⓒ Ⓓ   20. Ⓐ Ⓑ Ⓒ Ⓓ   26. Ⓐ Ⓑ Ⓒ Ⓓ
3. Ⓐ Ⓑ Ⓒ Ⓓ   9. Ⓐ Ⓑ Ⓒ Ⓓ   15. Ⓐ Ⓑ Ⓒ Ⓓ   21. Ⓐ Ⓑ Ⓒ Ⓓ   27. Ⓐ Ⓑ Ⓒ Ⓓ
4. Ⓐ Ⓑ Ⓒ Ⓓ   10. Ⓐ Ⓑ Ⓒ Ⓓ   16. Ⓐ Ⓑ Ⓒ Ⓓ   22. Ⓐ Ⓑ Ⓒ Ⓓ   28. Ⓐ Ⓑ Ⓒ Ⓓ
5. Ⓐ Ⓑ Ⓒ Ⓓ   11. Ⓐ Ⓑ Ⓒ Ⓓ   17. Ⓐ Ⓑ Ⓒ Ⓓ   23. Ⓐ Ⓑ Ⓒ Ⓓ   29. Ⓐ Ⓑ Ⓒ Ⓓ
6. Ⓐ Ⓑ Ⓒ Ⓓ   12. Ⓐ Ⓑ Ⓒ Ⓓ   18. Ⓐ Ⓑ Ⓒ Ⓓ   24. Ⓐ Ⓑ Ⓒ Ⓓ   30. Ⓐ Ⓑ Ⓒ Ⓓ

Name: _____ Date: _____

Standardized Testing   Answer Sheet

Unit Three: Mathematics   **Lesson Two: Computation (cont.)**

31. Ⓐ Ⓑ Ⓒ Ⓓ   37. Ⓐ Ⓑ Ⓒ Ⓓ   43. Ⓐ Ⓑ Ⓒ Ⓓ   49. Ⓐ Ⓑ Ⓒ Ⓓ   55. Ⓐ Ⓑ Ⓒ Ⓓ
32. Ⓐ Ⓑ Ⓒ Ⓓ   38. Ⓐ Ⓑ Ⓒ Ⓓ   44. Ⓐ Ⓑ Ⓒ Ⓓ   50. Ⓐ Ⓑ Ⓒ Ⓓ   56. Ⓐ Ⓑ Ⓒ Ⓓ
33. Ⓐ Ⓑ Ⓒ Ⓓ   39. Ⓐ Ⓑ Ⓒ Ⓓ   45. Ⓐ Ⓑ Ⓒ Ⓓ   51. Ⓐ Ⓑ Ⓒ Ⓓ   57. Ⓐ Ⓑ Ⓒ Ⓓ
34. Ⓐ Ⓑ Ⓒ Ⓓ   40. Ⓐ Ⓑ Ⓒ Ⓓ   46. Ⓐ Ⓑ Ⓒ Ⓓ   52. Ⓐ Ⓑ Ⓒ Ⓓ   58. Ⓐ Ⓑ Ⓒ Ⓓ
35. Ⓐ Ⓑ Ⓒ Ⓓ   41. Ⓐ Ⓑ Ⓒ Ⓓ   47. Ⓐ Ⓑ Ⓒ Ⓓ   53. Ⓐ Ⓑ Ⓒ Ⓓ   59. Ⓐ Ⓑ Ⓒ Ⓓ
36. Ⓐ Ⓑ Ⓒ Ⓓ   42. Ⓐ Ⓑ Ⓒ Ⓓ   48. Ⓐ Ⓑ Ⓒ Ⓓ   54. Ⓐ Ⓑ Ⓒ Ⓓ   60. Ⓐ Ⓑ Ⓒ Ⓓ

Unit Three: Mathematics   **Lesson Three: Problem Solving and Reasoning**

1. Ⓐ Ⓑ Ⓒ Ⓓ   8. Ⓐ Ⓑ Ⓒ Ⓓ   15. Ⓐ Ⓑ Ⓒ Ⓓ   22. Ⓐ Ⓑ Ⓒ Ⓓ   29. Ⓐ Ⓑ Ⓒ Ⓓ
2. Ⓐ Ⓑ Ⓒ Ⓓ   9. Ⓐ Ⓑ Ⓒ Ⓓ   16. Ⓐ Ⓑ Ⓒ Ⓓ   23. Ⓐ Ⓑ Ⓒ Ⓓ   30. Ⓐ Ⓑ Ⓒ Ⓓ
3. Ⓐ Ⓑ Ⓒ Ⓓ   10. Ⓐ Ⓑ Ⓒ Ⓓ   17. Ⓐ Ⓑ Ⓒ Ⓓ   24. Ⓐ Ⓑ Ⓒ Ⓓ   31. Ⓐ Ⓑ Ⓒ Ⓓ
4. Ⓐ Ⓑ Ⓒ Ⓓ   11. Ⓐ Ⓑ Ⓒ Ⓓ   18. Ⓐ Ⓑ Ⓒ Ⓓ   25. Ⓐ Ⓑ Ⓒ Ⓓ   32. Ⓐ Ⓑ Ⓒ Ⓓ
5. Ⓐ Ⓑ Ⓒ Ⓓ   12. Ⓐ Ⓑ Ⓒ Ⓓ   19. Ⓐ Ⓑ Ⓒ Ⓓ   26. Ⓐ Ⓑ Ⓒ Ⓓ   33. Ⓐ Ⓑ Ⓒ Ⓓ
6. Ⓐ Ⓑ Ⓒ Ⓓ   13. Ⓐ Ⓑ Ⓒ Ⓓ   20. Ⓐ Ⓑ Ⓒ Ⓓ   27. Ⓐ Ⓑ Ⓒ Ⓓ   34. Ⓐ Ⓑ Ⓒ Ⓓ
7. Ⓐ Ⓑ Ⓒ Ⓓ   14. Ⓐ Ⓑ Ⓒ Ⓓ   21. Ⓐ Ⓑ Ⓒ Ⓓ   28. Ⓐ Ⓑ Ⓒ Ⓓ   35. Ⓐ Ⓑ Ⓒ Ⓓ

Unit Four: Science   **Lesson One: Process and Inquiry**

1. Ⓐ Ⓑ Ⓒ Ⓓ   6. Ⓐ Ⓑ Ⓒ Ⓓ   11. Ⓐ Ⓑ Ⓒ Ⓓ   16. Ⓐ Ⓑ Ⓒ Ⓓ   21. Ⓐ Ⓑ Ⓒ Ⓓ
2. Ⓐ Ⓑ Ⓒ Ⓓ   7. Ⓐ Ⓑ Ⓒ Ⓓ   12. Ⓐ Ⓑ Ⓒ Ⓓ   17. Ⓐ Ⓑ Ⓒ Ⓓ   22. Ⓐ Ⓑ Ⓒ Ⓓ
3. Ⓐ Ⓑ Ⓒ Ⓓ   8. Ⓐ Ⓑ Ⓒ Ⓓ   13. Ⓐ Ⓑ Ⓒ Ⓓ   18. Ⓐ Ⓑ Ⓒ Ⓓ   23. Ⓐ Ⓑ Ⓒ Ⓓ
4. Ⓐ Ⓑ Ⓒ Ⓓ   9. Ⓐ Ⓑ Ⓒ Ⓓ   14. Ⓐ Ⓑ Ⓒ Ⓓ   19. Ⓐ Ⓑ Ⓒ Ⓓ   24. Ⓐ Ⓑ Ⓒ Ⓓ
5. Ⓐ Ⓑ Ⓒ Ⓓ   10. Ⓐ Ⓑ Ⓒ Ⓓ   15. Ⓐ Ⓑ Ⓒ Ⓓ   20. Ⓐ Ⓑ Ⓒ Ⓓ   25. Ⓐ Ⓑ Ⓒ Ⓓ

Unit Four: Science   **Lesson Two: Concepts**

1. Ⓐ Ⓑ Ⓒ Ⓓ   9. Ⓐ Ⓑ Ⓒ Ⓓ   17. Ⓐ Ⓑ Ⓒ Ⓓ   25. Ⓐ Ⓑ Ⓒ Ⓓ   33. Ⓐ Ⓑ Ⓒ Ⓓ
2. Ⓐ Ⓑ Ⓒ Ⓓ   10. Ⓐ Ⓑ Ⓒ Ⓓ   18. Ⓐ Ⓑ Ⓒ Ⓓ   26. Ⓐ Ⓑ Ⓒ Ⓓ   34. Ⓐ Ⓑ Ⓒ Ⓓ
3. Ⓐ Ⓑ Ⓒ Ⓓ   11. Ⓐ Ⓑ Ⓒ Ⓓ   19. Ⓐ Ⓑ Ⓒ Ⓓ   27. Ⓐ Ⓑ Ⓒ Ⓓ   35. Ⓐ Ⓑ Ⓒ Ⓓ
4. Ⓐ Ⓑ Ⓒ Ⓓ   12. Ⓐ Ⓑ Ⓒ Ⓓ   20. Ⓐ Ⓑ Ⓒ Ⓓ   28. Ⓐ Ⓑ Ⓒ Ⓓ   36. Ⓐ Ⓑ Ⓒ Ⓓ
5. Ⓐ Ⓑ Ⓒ Ⓓ   13. Ⓐ Ⓑ Ⓒ Ⓓ   21. Ⓐ Ⓑ Ⓒ Ⓓ   29. Ⓐ Ⓑ Ⓒ Ⓓ   37. Ⓐ Ⓑ Ⓒ Ⓓ
6. Ⓐ Ⓑ Ⓒ Ⓓ   14. Ⓐ Ⓑ Ⓒ Ⓓ   22. Ⓐ Ⓑ Ⓒ Ⓓ   30. Ⓐ Ⓑ Ⓒ Ⓓ   38. Ⓐ Ⓑ Ⓒ Ⓓ
7. Ⓐ Ⓑ Ⓒ Ⓓ   15. Ⓐ Ⓑ Ⓒ Ⓓ   23. Ⓐ Ⓑ Ⓒ Ⓓ   31. Ⓐ Ⓑ Ⓒ Ⓓ   39. Ⓐ Ⓑ Ⓒ Ⓓ
8. Ⓐ Ⓑ Ⓒ Ⓓ   16. Ⓐ Ⓑ Ⓒ Ⓓ   24. Ⓐ Ⓑ Ⓒ Ⓓ   32. Ⓐ Ⓑ Ⓒ Ⓓ   40. Ⓐ Ⓑ Ⓒ Ⓓ

Name: _____   Date: _____

Standardized Testing Grade 5 Answer Sheet

Unit Five: Social Studies   **Lesson One: History and Culture**

1. Ⓐ Ⓑ Ⓒ Ⓓ   9. Ⓐ Ⓑ Ⓒ Ⓓ   17. Ⓐ Ⓑ Ⓒ Ⓓ   25. Ⓐ Ⓑ Ⓒ Ⓓ   33. Ⓐ Ⓑ Ⓒ Ⓓ
2. Ⓐ Ⓑ Ⓒ Ⓓ   10. Ⓐ Ⓑ Ⓒ Ⓓ   18. Ⓐ Ⓑ Ⓒ Ⓓ   26. Ⓐ Ⓑ Ⓒ Ⓓ   34. Ⓐ Ⓑ Ⓒ Ⓓ
3. Ⓐ Ⓑ Ⓒ Ⓓ   11. Ⓐ Ⓑ Ⓒ Ⓓ   19. Ⓐ Ⓑ Ⓒ Ⓓ   27. Ⓐ Ⓑ Ⓒ Ⓓ   35. Ⓐ Ⓑ Ⓒ Ⓓ
4. Ⓐ Ⓑ Ⓒ Ⓓ   12. Ⓐ Ⓑ Ⓒ Ⓓ   20. Ⓐ Ⓑ Ⓒ Ⓓ   28. Ⓐ Ⓑ Ⓒ Ⓓ   36. Ⓐ Ⓑ Ⓒ Ⓓ
5. Ⓐ Ⓑ Ⓒ Ⓓ   13. Ⓐ Ⓑ Ⓒ Ⓓ   21. Ⓐ Ⓑ Ⓒ Ⓓ   29. Ⓐ Ⓑ Ⓒ Ⓓ   37. Ⓐ Ⓑ Ⓒ Ⓓ
6. Ⓐ Ⓑ Ⓒ Ⓓ   14. Ⓐ Ⓑ Ⓒ Ⓓ   22. Ⓐ Ⓑ Ⓒ Ⓓ   30. Ⓐ Ⓑ Ⓒ Ⓓ   38. Ⓐ Ⓑ Ⓒ Ⓓ
7. Ⓐ Ⓑ Ⓒ Ⓓ   15. Ⓐ Ⓑ Ⓒ Ⓓ   23. Ⓐ Ⓑ Ⓒ Ⓓ   31. Ⓐ Ⓑ Ⓒ Ⓓ   39. Ⓐ Ⓑ Ⓒ Ⓓ
8. Ⓐ Ⓑ Ⓒ Ⓓ   16. Ⓐ Ⓑ Ⓒ Ⓓ   24. Ⓐ Ⓑ Ⓒ Ⓓ   32. Ⓐ Ⓑ Ⓒ Ⓓ   40. Ⓐ Ⓑ Ⓒ Ⓓ

Unit Five: Social Studies   **Lesson Two: Civics, Government, and Economics**

1. Ⓐ Ⓑ Ⓒ Ⓓ   7. Ⓐ Ⓑ Ⓒ Ⓓ   13. Ⓐ Ⓑ Ⓒ Ⓓ   19. Ⓐ Ⓑ Ⓒ Ⓓ   25. Ⓐ Ⓑ Ⓒ Ⓓ
2. Ⓐ Ⓑ Ⓒ Ⓓ   8. Ⓐ Ⓑ Ⓒ Ⓓ   14. Ⓐ Ⓑ Ⓒ Ⓓ   20. Ⓐ Ⓑ Ⓒ Ⓓ   26. Ⓐ Ⓑ Ⓒ Ⓓ
3. Ⓐ Ⓑ Ⓒ Ⓓ   9. Ⓐ Ⓑ Ⓒ Ⓓ   15. Ⓐ Ⓑ Ⓒ Ⓓ   21. Ⓐ Ⓑ Ⓒ Ⓓ   27. Ⓐ Ⓑ Ⓒ Ⓓ
4. Ⓐ Ⓑ Ⓒ Ⓓ   10. Ⓐ Ⓑ Ⓒ Ⓓ   16. Ⓐ Ⓑ Ⓒ Ⓓ   22. Ⓐ Ⓑ Ⓒ Ⓓ   28. Ⓐ Ⓑ Ⓒ Ⓓ
5. Ⓐ Ⓑ Ⓒ Ⓓ   11. Ⓐ Ⓑ Ⓒ Ⓓ   17. Ⓐ Ⓑ Ⓒ Ⓓ   23. Ⓐ Ⓑ Ⓒ Ⓓ   29. Ⓐ Ⓑ Ⓒ Ⓓ
6. Ⓐ Ⓑ Ⓒ Ⓓ   12. Ⓐ Ⓑ Ⓒ Ⓓ   18. Ⓐ Ⓑ Ⓒ Ⓓ   24. Ⓐ Ⓑ Ⓒ Ⓓ   30. Ⓐ Ⓑ Ⓒ Ⓓ

Unit Five: Social Studies   **Lesson Three: Geography**

1. Ⓐ Ⓑ Ⓒ Ⓓ   8. Ⓐ Ⓑ Ⓒ Ⓓ   15. Ⓐ Ⓑ Ⓒ Ⓓ   22. Ⓐ Ⓑ Ⓒ Ⓓ   29. Ⓐ Ⓑ Ⓒ Ⓓ
2. Ⓐ Ⓑ Ⓒ Ⓓ   9. Ⓐ Ⓑ Ⓒ Ⓓ   16. Ⓐ Ⓑ Ⓒ Ⓓ   23. Ⓐ Ⓑ Ⓒ Ⓓ   30. Ⓐ Ⓑ Ⓒ Ⓓ
3. Ⓐ Ⓑ Ⓒ Ⓓ   10. Ⓐ Ⓑ Ⓒ Ⓓ   17. Ⓐ Ⓑ Ⓒ Ⓓ   24. Ⓐ Ⓑ Ⓒ Ⓓ   31. Ⓐ Ⓑ Ⓒ Ⓓ
4. Ⓐ Ⓑ Ⓒ Ⓓ   11. Ⓐ Ⓑ Ⓒ Ⓓ   18. Ⓐ Ⓑ Ⓒ Ⓓ   25. Ⓐ Ⓑ Ⓒ Ⓓ   32. Ⓐ Ⓑ Ⓒ Ⓓ
5. Ⓐ Ⓑ Ⓒ Ⓓ   12. Ⓐ Ⓑ Ⓒ Ⓓ   19. Ⓐ Ⓑ Ⓒ Ⓓ   26. Ⓐ Ⓑ Ⓒ Ⓓ   33. Ⓐ Ⓑ Ⓒ Ⓓ
6. Ⓐ Ⓑ Ⓒ Ⓓ   13. Ⓐ Ⓑ Ⓒ Ⓓ   20. Ⓐ Ⓑ Ⓒ Ⓓ   27. Ⓐ Ⓑ Ⓒ Ⓓ   34. Ⓐ Ⓑ Ⓒ Ⓓ
7. Ⓐ Ⓑ Ⓒ Ⓓ   14. Ⓐ Ⓑ Ⓒ Ⓓ   21. Ⓐ Ⓑ Ⓒ Ⓓ   28. Ⓐ Ⓑ Ⓒ Ⓓ   35. Ⓐ Ⓑ Ⓒ Ⓓ

Standardized Testing Grade 5 Answer Key

School:	Student Name		
Teacher:	Last	First	MI

Female ◯ **Male** ◯

Birth Date

Month	Day	Year
Jan ◯	⓪ ⓪	⓪ ⓪
Feb ◯	① ①	① ①
Mar ◯	② ②	② ②
Apr ◯	③ ③	③ ③
May ◯	④	④ ④
Jun ◯	⑤	⑤ ⑤
Jul ◯	⑥	⑥ ⑥
Aug ◯	⑦	⑦ ⑦
Sep ◯	⑧	⑧ ⑧
Oct ◯	⑨	⑨ ⑨
Nov ◯		
Dec ◯		

Grade
③ ④ ⑤ ⑥ ⑦ ⑧

Unit One: Reading   Lesson One: Vocabulary

1. C	10. D	19. A	28. A	37. C
2. A	11. B	20. A	29. D	38. A
3. B	12. C	21. C	30. A	39. D
4. B	13. C	22. B	31. A	40. C
5. A	14. A	23. D	32. B	41. A
6. D	15. B	24. B	33. A	42. B
7. B	16. B	25. A	34. D	43. B
8. A	17. C	26. C	35. A	44. D
9. C	18. B	27. B	36. A	45. C

Standardized Testing Grade 5 Answer Key

Unit One: Reading   Lesson Two: Word Analysis

#	Ans	#	Ans	#	Ans	#	Ans	#	Ans
1	C	13	C	25	B	37	C	49	D
2	D	14	A	26	B	38	B	50	B
3	C	15	C	27	C	39	A	51	C
4	D	16	B	28	B	40	A	52	B
5	C	17	D	29	A	41	C	53	C
6	C	18	D	30	C	42	C	54	B
7	C	19	B	31	B	43	D	55	B
8	B	20	A	32	D	44	A	56	A
9	C	21	C	33	B	45	B	57	B
10	D	22	D	34	D	46	C	58	C
11	B	23	A	35	C	47	D	59	B
12	A	24	B	36	D	48	C	60	C

Unit One: Reading   Lesson Three: Comprehension

#	Ans	#	Ans	#	Ans	#	Ans	#	Ans
1	A	11	A	21	C	31	B	41	B
2	B	12	C	22	B	32	A	42	C
3	B	13	C	23	C	33	B	43	C
4	C	14	C	24	C	34	C	44	D
5	C	15	B	25	A	35	B	45	D
6	D	16	C	26	D	36	D	46	B
7	B	17	D	27	B	37	A	47	C
8	C	18	C	28	A	38	B	48	C
9	D	19	A	29	C	39	B	49	B
10	A	20	D	30	D	40	A	50	A

Unit Two: Language   Lesson One: Mechanics

#	Ans	#	Ans	#	Ans	#	Ans	#	Ans
1	B	8	C	15	C	22	B	29	C
2	D	9	C	16	C	23	C	30	D
3	C	10	A	17	B	24	D	31	B
4	B	11	B	18	C	25	C	32	A
5	A	12	B	19	A	26	D	33	A
6	B	13	A	20	B	27	B	34	B
7	D	14	C	21	C	28	A	35	C

Standardized Testing Grade 5 Answer Key

Unit Two: Language   Lesson Two: Expression

1. C
2. A
3. D
4. B
5. C
6. A
7. B
8. A
9. A
10. D
11. C
12. B
13. C
14. B
15. B
16. D
17. A
18. A
19. C
20. C
21. A
22. B
23. D
24. B
25. B

Unit Two: Language   Lesson Three: Information Skills

1. C
2. A
3. C
4. D
5. B
6. B
7. C
8. D
9. C
10. B
11. D
12. A
13. D
14. B
15. C
16. B
17. A
18. D
19. A
20. D
21. C
22. B
23. D
24. A
25. C
26. A
27. D
28. B
29. C
30. D

Unit Three: Mathematics   Lesson One: Concepts

1. B
2. D
3. A
4. C
5. A
6. B
7. C
8. D
9. C
10. D
11. C
12. C
13. A
14. C
15. D
16. D
17. A
18. D
19. A
20. C
21. B
22. B
23. D
24. A
25. B
26. B
27. D
28. A
29. C
30. C
31. A
32. D
33. B
34. B
35. C
36. C
37. A
38. C
39. D
40. A
41. C
42. B
43. B
44. A
45. B
46. D
47. B
48. D
49. B
50. B

Unit Three: Mathematics   Lesson Two: Computation

1. B
2. D
3. C
4. A
5. C
6. D
7. C
8. D
9. C
10. A
11. C
12. C
13. C
14. B
15. D
16. B
17. A
18. C
19. D
20. B
21. B
22. C
23. D
24. B
25. C
26. C
27. C
28. A
29. C
30. B

Standardized Testing Grade 5 Answer Key

Unit Three: Mathematics   **Lesson Two: Computation (cont.)**

31. A	37. C	43. A	49. C	55. C
32. B	38. A	44. B	50. A	56. A
33. C	39. B	45. B	51. B	57. D
34. D	40. B	46. A	52. D	58. A
35. C	41. C	47. C	53. B	59. A
36. C	42. A	48. A	54. A	60. A

Unit Three: Mathematics   **Lesson Three: Problem Solving and Reasoning**

1. A	8. A	15. B	22. A	29. D
2. C	9. C	16. C	23. C	30. D
3. B	10. B	17. D	24. B	31. D
4. A	11. C	18. C	25. B	32. D
5. C	12. A	19. A	26. B	33. C
6. B	13. B	20. A	27. B	34. C
7. B	14. A	21. B	28. A	35. D

Unit Four: Science   **Lesson One: Process and Inquiry**

1. A	6. B	11. C	16. C	21. D
2. A	7. D	12. C	17. C	22. B
3. C	8. C	13. A	18. C	23. D
4. A	9. A	14. D	19. A	24. C
5. B	10. C	15. D	20. C	25. D

Unit Four: Science   **Lesson Two: Concepts**

1. C	9. B	17. A	25. A	33. D
2. A	10. B	18. B	26. B	34. A
3. D	11. A	19. B	27. B	35. B
4. B	12. C	20. A	28. C	36. B
5. A	13. A	21. D	29. A	37. A
6. D	14. B	22. B	30. C	38. A
7. B	15. A	23. C	31. C	39. C
8. B	16. C	24. D	32. A	40. D

Standardized Testing Grade 5 Answer Key

Unit Five: Social Studies   Lesson One: History and Culture

1. B	9. D	17. B	25. A	33. B
2. A	10. C	18. D	26. C	34. A
3. D	11. A	19. A	27. A	35. D
4. B	12. C	20. C	28. C	36. C
5. C	13. C	21. B	29. A	37. A
6. C	14. A	22. B	30. C	38. C
7. B	15. C	23. C	31. C	39. B
8. A	16. C	24. D	32. C	40. C

Unit Five: Social Studies   Lesson Two: Civics, Government, and Economics

1. D	7. D	13. A	19. C	25. C
2. A	8. A	14. D	20. D	26. B
3. C	9. B	15. A	21. B	27. C
4. B	10. D	16. B	22. C	28. A
5. C	11. C	17. C	23. B	29. D
6. A	12. B	18. B	24. A	30. C

Unit Five: Social Studies   Lesson Three: Geography

1. C	8. C	15. A	22. A	29. A
2. B	9. B	16. B	23. C	30. B
3. D	10. A	17. C	24. B	31. C
4. C	11. B	18. D	25. A	32. D
5. C	12. C	19. A	26. B	33. A
6. A	13. B	20. B	27. D	34. D
7. A	14. C	21. D	28. C	35. C